THE AMERICAN
FACT•IONARY

The Easy Way to Enhance Your Vocabulary & Writing Skills

S.J. TESTA

Includes Intriguing Facts That Will Enrich Your Life

TATE PUBLISHING & *Enterprises*

For My Three Sons: Mike, Troy and Jim

*Who from the day each entered this world,
have been never-ending sources
of joy, love and pride*

Acknowledgements

Recognition is given to a group of "amateur editors" who, with sharp pencils in hand, willingly gave their time to make the manuscript better. They are: Amy Bollman, Al & Joyce Amanda Testa, Mary Buckalew, and Bob & Vicki Edge. To my friends at Bent Tree who read the initial drafts and made sound recommendations and suggestions. They are: Jim Goodnight, Chris Cree and Kim Macalik. And finally, to the sounding boards throughout the project in the persons of my sons, Mike, Troy and Jim, and their friend and my friend, Dave Erdman. A heartfelt thanks to all.

Foreword
By Gloria Gannaway, Ph.D.

It's very refreshing when people who aren't "certified experts" decide to share what they know—they often know quite a lot; moreover, they often have an interestingly different perspective, not having been hammered into a mold by establishment training! It is such an offering you now hold in your hands—*The American Fact•ionary*, written by someone who writes well, loves words, and has learned a thing or two in the professional trenches over the years that he would like to share with you to help you in your never-ending struggle to be a better writer. And if you think I've exaggerated, stop a moment and think how you feel every time you have to submit a report or write an important letter or email. A little anxiety, and a lack of confidence, perhaps, about using the right words and expressing yourself clearly, precisely, and effectively?

There are many aids for writers, most written by the pros, and probably all of them are useful. Most of us, though, don't get around to consulting them—we just do the best we can and hope for the best, usually with the uneasy feeling that we could have and should have done better. Testa has provided us with an accessible little volume of useful words, facts, and writing tips that we can carry around with us and digest in small snacks, thus painlessly improving our writing little by little. As he points out, this isn't the be-all end-all writer's guide. In some ways, it's more than that—it's one person's compilation of words and tidbits, gathered from his own experiences, that you can pick and choose from. Once you've got the hang of it, you can add to it on your own. It goes great with a cup of coffee!

It does this writing teacher's heart good to introduce this little gem to one and all—college students who suddenly find themselves swamped with daunting writing assignments; new graduates taking on the challenges of the first job; as well as seasoned professionals who haven't learned a new word or spiffed up their writing styles in decades. That Testa isn't a professional writer or teacher conveys a message and a lesson in itself - it says that everyone can and should take writing seriously, and that sometimes the best teachers are just those who care enough to pass on what they've learned.

* Dr. Gannaway holds a Ph.D in English/Rhetoric and is a teacher and published author. She was most recently a Professor at the Institute of North American Studies in Barcelona, Spain. She currently teaches professional English for International House in Barcelona and is a researcher/writer in the Department of Technology and Education at the University of Barcelona.

PREFACE

Being able to write well by using the right words in clear and concisely crafted sentences is not a difficult assignment once you learn a few key fundamentals. Most of us already know the basic grammar and punctuation rules like starting a sentence with the first letter capitalized and ending the sentence with a period. It's what happens between the two that requires some attention.

The American Fact•ionary focuses on this middle ground by enhancing your writing skills and expanding your vocabulary with specifically chosen words from the dictionary as the framework for its presentation.

Initially, the information contained herein was intended to be a personal gift to my sons, a gift that in some small way might help to expand and enrich their lives. However, not long after the project began, one of them suggested that it should be prepared for a larger audience.

It is important to note that I am neither a lexicographer nor an etymologist, but merely an individual with an abiding respect for both the beauty and versatility of the English language, notwithstanding some of its quirks and irregularities.

As human beings, we differ from other animals on the planet in that we have ideas and the ability to express those ideas with words. Using the right words that clearly communicate our intentions will often-times dictate success or failure.

The words included herein are not $25 words designed to make you appear as an intellectual. They are $10 words that you should know and use; words that should be included in your conversations, letters, e-mails, marketing presentations, proposals, essays, and reports; words that will remarkably increase the effectiveness of your verbal and written communications.

For the most part, the words are in alphabetical order. However, when certain words are commonly confused with other words, I have placed them together to make it easier to understand the differences in their meanings.

Interspersed among the definitions is information on certain people, places and events that you probably have heard about, but know little about; fascinating items that will captivate your interest and expand your mind. As a result, I have called this document a "fact•ionary" since it includes interesting facts that surround our lives and specifically chosen words from the dictionary.

Building A Vocabulary

Building a decent vocabulary is not as daunting an undertaking as one might think. It's the size of a typical unabridged dictionary that raises eyebrows. There are a few inquisitive souls who have actually read a dictionary from cover to cover, but most of us are reading other materials for either business, educational or entertainment purposes. Reading a dictionary is tedious work. Normally, we go there only to look up word definitions or verify spellings. While a lot of us have occasionally listened to vocabulary tapes or read vocabulary books, we typically build our vocabularies and write grammatically correct sentences by hearing and reading words in context.

There is, however, a way to accelerate and enhance the process. If you take the average sized unabridged dictionary and remove all of the words that pertain to specific disciplines such as, religion, astronomy, physics, chemistry, zoology, medicine, music, biological sciences, computer sciences, engineering, geography, philosophy, to name a few, you will reduce the dictionary to roughly half its size. Next, remove all common and well-known words like, "car," "street," " house," "cat," "dog," and the like, and another large portion of the dictionary disappears. What remains are words previously referred to as $25 words and $10 words. The $25 words can be long, multi-syllable words that we may have heard or seen, but most of us have no idea what they mean. Words like "abscissions" or "intenerations" fall into this category. They can also be much shorter words that are just as obscure and infrequently used as their longer counterparts. These are words like "col," "gat," or "fub." Good words, one and all, but we will entrust these shorter words to the Scrabble players. The final cut then is to remove the longer $25 words, but don't discard them completely. Put them in safekeeping to be called upon only on those rare occasions when no other word adequately expresses the point you want to make. What remains now is a relatively small number of $10 words. The focus of *The American Fact•ionary* is on these $10 words. These are the words you should learn, know and use if you want to write well and communicate effectively.

Reportedly, there is an interesting anecdote concerning American novelist, Ernest Hemingway, who is well known for having used short words in tersely written sentences. (From *Big Two-Hearted River:* "Nick laughed. He would finish the cigarette. The river was there.") Commenting on some of Hemingway's work, fellow novelist William Faulkner stated that "He has never been known to use a word that might send a reader to the dictionary." To which Hemingway is said to have replied, "Poor Faulkner. Does he really think big emotions come from big words? He thinks I don't know the [$25 words]. I know them all right. But there are older and simpler and better words, and those are the ones I use." They should be the ones we all use when clarity and understanding are the ultimate rewards for good writing.

Changes To The SAT

In 2005, the College Board, concerned over the poor state of affairs of writing in America, announced major changes to the SAT. The board had previously established the National Commission of Writing for America's Families, Schools, and Colleges. These efforts were undertaken to focus national attention on the need to enhance writing skills in America. The new SAT will now require a twenty-five-minute written essay that must effectively communicate a viewpoint that defines and supports a position. This requirement will be coupled with a thirty-five-minute multiple-choice section. Of the two hundred and twenty minutes required to take the scored portion of the SAT, a full sixty minutes will now be devoted to writing and verbal skills. The commission issued a report called,

"Writing: A Ticket To Work. . . . Or A Ticket Out." It concludes that the ability to write opens doors to professional employment and that those unable to express themselves clearly will have limited opportunities. The report boldly states, "If students want professional work in service firms, in banking, finance, insurance, and real estate, they must know how to communicate on paper clearly and concisely." Learning how to use the right words in clear and concisely crafted sentences is the essence of *The American Fact•ionary*.

—S. J. Testa

REFERENCES

Oxford English Reference Dictionary, 2nd Edition, Revised. Oxford University Press.

The American College Dictionary. Random House.

Roget's International Thesaurus, 4th Edition. Harper & Row, Publishers, Inc.

Merriam-Webster's Online Dictionary, 10th Edition

Dictionary. com

Hyperdictionary. com

Cambridge International Dictionary of English

The American Heritage Dictionary of the English Language

Dictionary of Quotations. Chartwell Books, Inc.

Put Downs: A Collection of Acid Wit. PRC Publishing Limited

"My father still reads the dictionary every day. He says your life depends on your power to master words."

Arthur Scargill, British trade union leader
Sunday Times, Jan. 10, 1982

THE AMERICAN
FACT•IONARY

A.M. & P.M.
> (Latin) For *ante meridiem* and *post meridiem*.
> It means "before noon" and "after noon."

ABATE
(uh **bait**)
> *Verb.* To decrease. To become less intense. To subside. That which is progressively diminishing. To wane. To become less forceful. Declining.
>
> • *To the regret of its inhabitants, the fighting has not* **abated** *in this small war-torn country.*
>
> • *His work continually met with critical resistance that showed no signs of* **abatement** (**noun form**) *until he won the Pulitzer Prize.*

ABIDING
(uh **bye** ding)
> *Adj.* That which is long lasting. Enduring. Steadfast. Continual and unchanging. That which is unshakable. Unceasing.

• He has an **abiding** belief that the most important quality of a human being is to have respect for others.

• Her most **abiding** memory from those youthful days is of her mother reading to her in the evenings before it was time to go to bed.

• He has had an **abiding** love of music since he was a young child.

ABSTRUSE
(ab **struse**)

Adj. **Difficult to understand. Puzzling. Complex. Baffling. Hard to comprehend. Confusing. Cryptic. Recondite. Perplexing. Not comprehensible for one of ordinary knowledge or understanding.**

• *Oftentimes, he would attempt to impress his colleagues by introducing profound and* **abstruse** *topics of discussion.*

• *He had no interest in the study of quantum mechanics—that branch of quantum physics that accounts for matter at the atomic level. It was simply too* **abstruse** *and difficult to understand.*

✪   The opposite of "abstruse" is "simple."

ACERBITY
(uh **sir** buh tee)

Noun. **Sourness. Astringency of taste. Bitter. Sharp. Tartness. By extension the word is more commonly used to indicate a harshness or sever-**

ity of someone's language, expression, or temper. Showing acrimony. That which is vicious. Cruel or harsh.

• *We knew he was upset, but the acerbity with which he responded to the news surprised us all.*

• *He was both loved and feared for the acerbity of his wit.*

• *He was an editorial writer for the newspaper who gained status as an acerbic (adjectival form), ill-tempered observer of the human condition.*

ACQUIESCE
(ak we es)

Verb. To agree. To comply. To submit tacitly. To give in or yield. To concede. To agree by failing to object. To assent. To yield without protest. To give consent.

• *The chairman stood by his previous decision not to acquiesce to the demands made by members of the local labor union.*

• *Although he was tired, the singing sensation acquiesced to a request for an encore.*

✪   The opposite of "acquiesce" is "resist" or "hold firm."

AD HOC
(ad **hock**)

(Latin) Literally "to this." For a special purpose. With respect to a particular subject or thing. For this topic only. To provide temporary solutions to a problem. Either politically or corporately in response to a problem or condition.

• *We typically solve a lot of our problems on an **ad hoc** basis.*

• *The Board of Directors recommended the establishment of an **ad hoc** committee to study the issue of management compensation.*

• *We should develop an ongoing strategy that we can execute rather than continually relying on a series of **ad hoc** decisions.*

ADJUDICATE
(uh **jew** duh kate)

Verb. **To judge. To deliver a judgment. To settle by decree. To come to a judicial decision. To resolve. To give a ruling. To decide.**

• *It was a fiercely contested land dispute between wealthy landowners that was **adjudicated** in court.*

• *They formed a military tribunal charged with the responsibility of **adjudicating** those cases involving military personnel.*

AUTHOR'S NOTE
One of the more interesting cases ever adjudicated in the United States occurred in the late 1800s over the issue of whether a tomato is a fruit or a vegetable. Because of existing import tariffs in force at the time, it was necessary to call the tomato one or the other. Incredibly, the case ended up in the United States Supreme Court where the court ruled that even though tomatoes are considered a fruit of the vine, they are commonly eaten with the main meal much like lettuce, carrots, celery, etc., while fruits are typically eaten as a dessert. Thus, the tomato officially became a vegetable.

ALLUSION
(uh **loo** zhen)

> *Noun.* **A reference to something supposedly well known. A suggestion or insinuation. An implied or indirect reference. Something that is hinted at or referred to. A reference to a person, place, or thing that is widely known.**
>
> • *The book contains only a brief **allusion** to his boyhood days in the South.*
>
> • *Without naming names, he **alluded** (verb form) to the improprieties that had occurred at the White House.*

> ### Author's note
> A much-used allusion is the phrase "Draconian measures." This phrase is an allusion to the harsh and unusual punishment given to those who broke the laws as stipulated by Draco, the first to legislate the laws of ancient Greece. Oftentimes, offenders were put to death for even minor infractions. Thus, the word "Draconian" is used as an allusion to harsh and unusual activity.

Do not confuse "allusion" with the noun "illusion" (il **loo** zhen). An illusion is a misleading impression; one that defies conventional explanation; one that distorts any of our sensory perceptions; a deceptive activity.

• *Even though he accomplished very little, he spent many hours in the library, and it gave the **illusion** that he was studying hard.*

• *David Copperfield is a widely acclaimed **illusionist**.*

AMBIGUOUS
(am **big** u us)

Adj. Vague. Unclear or uncertain. Doubtful. Open to two or more possible meanings. Indistinct. Obscure or indefinite. Equivocal. That which can be interpreted differently. Imprecise.

• *Our attorney thought the wording of the agreement was too **ambiguous**.*

• *In certain psychological tests, the stimuli employed to provoke responses are intentionally* **ambiguous** *to allow for those being tested to project their own personal and unique reactions.*

• *Some of the questions on the test were either poorly or* **ambiguously** (adverbial form) *written.*

The noun form of "ambiguous" is "ambiguity" (am buh **gue** a tee). **It means uncertainty or doubtfulness. It is a condition lacking clarity.**

• *The President's speech should be free of all* **ambiguities***.*

✪ The opposite of "ambiguous" is "clear" or "precise."

AMELIORATE
(uh **meal** yuh **rate**)

Verb. **To make better or to grow better. To improve. To meliorate. To make a bad condition or situation better. To ease. To alleviate or to assuage. To make something more bearable.**

• *The new medicine will help to* **ameliorate** *his condition.*

• *More heating oil will be required to* **ameliorate** *the effects of the wintry conditions in the Northeast.*

AMISS
(uh **miss**)

> *Adj./Adv.* **In an incorrect or improper manner. Wrong. Muddled. Faulty. Inappropriate. Gone awry.**
>
> • *You judge* **amiss** *if you think he is not capable of such misconduct.*
>
> • *In his wonderful essay entitled* Walter Benjamin at the Dairy Queen, *Larry McMurtry reflects on the speed and celerity with which his grandmother could prepare a chicken dinner: "She would simply whirl the chicken around a few times and pop off its head. Often a pullet would be killed, plucked, cut up, and cooked before the head quite realized that something was seriously* **amiss.**"

ANAGRAM
(**ann** uh **gram**)

> *Noun.* **A transposition of letters in a word to form a new word.**
>
> • *"Eat" can become "tea." "Tire" can become "rite."*

ANCILLARY
(**an** suh **lair** ee)

> *Adj.* **Accompanying. Supplemental. That which is attendant. Something added, but not essential. Contributory. Auxiliary or secondary.**
>
> • *We were provided with workbooks, handouts, and other* **ancillary** *items to be used in conjunction with the basic textbook.*

> • *Even though he was involved with the campaign, he played only an* **ancillary** *role in the senator's bid for re-election.*

> • *The CEO wanted to tour the main manufacturing facility and its* **ancillary** *plants.*

✪   The opposite of "ancillary" is "main."

ANOMALY
(uh **nom** uh lee)

> *Noun.* **A person or thing that is different from what is common. Abnormal. Different from what is expected. Something unusual. Irregular. That which deviates from the standard. Peculiar. An oddity. An aberration. Different from what is typical.**

> • *He was loud and garrulous and certainly an* **anomaly** *in a family of quiet, soft spoken individuals.*

> • *There is a direct correlation between* **anomalies** *in the surface temperatures of the planet's oceans and irregular changes in climate.*

ANTE-
Word element meaning "before."

ANTEBELLUM
(**ann** tee **bell** em)

> *Adj.* **Before the war (Civil). Also, a type or style of old house.**

• *The book is a brilliant study of social history from the* **antebellum** *period through reconstruction.*

ANTEDILUVIAN
(**ann** tee da **loo** vee un)

Adj. **Before the deluge or flood. The word means old or antiquated.**

• *In the meeting, he was of little help. He offered only* **antediluvian** *ideas and concepts.*

• *With a twinkle in his eye, the wise, old professor asked the students in his class to refrain from calling him "the* **antediluvian** *advisor."*

ANTITHESIS
(ann **tith** uh sis)

Noun. **The exact opposite. In opposition. Contrast. The direct opposite.**

• *Her ideas are the* **antithesis** *of mine.*

• *He is the* **antithesis** *of the type of man I most admire.*

• *The threat of global terrorism has lessened the importance of the political* **antithesis** *between liberals and conservatives.*

The word is also a figure of speech that puts together contrasting ideas to produce a rhetorical effect. In a single sentence, it is an expression emphasizing opposing ideas or actions as shown in the following:

• *Out with the old, in with the new.*

• *What goes up must come down.*

• *"Give me liberty, or give me death."* (Patrick Henry)

Do not confuse "antithesis" with the noun "antipathy." "Antipathy" means a strong dislike. It is something that is repugnant, revolting, or disgusting. It is a source of hostility.

• *She was a reclusive writer with a deep **antipathy** for the press.*

APHORISM
(**af** or **riz** em)

> *Noun.* **A short, brief statement of an accepted truth. A maxim. A saying. The following are well known aphorisms:**

• *"Waste not, want not."*

• *"A penny saved is a penny earned."*

• *"Make hay while the sun shines."*

APPRISE
(uh **prize**)

> *Verb.* **To tell. To give notice. To inform. To advise or notify. To explain. To disclose or report.**

• *The comptroller **apprised** the CFO that an accounting error had been made.*

• *She has been* **apprised** *of her rights.*

Do not confuse "apprise" with "appraise" (uh praze). **"Appraise" is a verb meaning to evaluate or assess. To estimate. To gauge. To determine the value of.**

• *His grandfather's pocket watch had been* **appraised** *at over a thousand dollars.*

ASCETIC
(ass **set** ik)

Adj. **A rigid, sparse existence. Doing without. Abstaining or abstemious. Living a simple life for religious purposes. Austere. Self-denial especially of material comforts.**

• *He was a member of a religious sect that led very* **ascetic** *lives.*

• *Collegiate wrestlers are, by comparison, an* **ascetic** *bunch, avoiding bad, unhealthy habits and continually fighting to maintain their weight.*

ASSIDUOUS
(uh **sij** u ous)

Adj. **Constant. Unremitting. Incessant. Non-abating. Continual diligence. Relentless and persistent.**

• *His* **assiduous** *efforts insured his success.*

• *He has been remarkably* **assiduous** *in his attempts to enhance his marketing skills.*

*• No one should be surprised at her accomplishments. She has always **assiduously** (adverbial form) applied herself to her studies.*

AVOCATION
(**av** o **kay** shen)

> *Noun.* **The primary meaning of this word is something an individual does in addition to his or her primary occupation. A hobby. Something done for pleasure. A diversion or distraction. An auxiliary or spare time activity.**
>
> *• Her vocation is practicing law, but her **avocation** is playing the cello.*
>
> **The secondary meaning of "avocation" is an individual's regular occupation, calling, or career. In this regard, the secondary definition of "avocation" means the same as the word "vocation" (your profession, job, or means of livelihood). To avoid confusion on the reader's part, some usage arbiters recommend restricting the use of the word "avocation" to mean hobby or pastime and the word "vocation" to mean occupation.**

BEDROCK
(**bed rock**)

> *Noun.* **Formations of solid rock beneath the soil. Gravel or rock fragments. By extension, the word is used to mean any solid foundation. A Base. An Underpinning.**
>
> *• There are those who believe that impressions found in*

*the limestone **bedrock** along certain streams and rivers in Texas are footprints of humans and prove they existed contemporaneously with dinosaurs.*

• *The family unit is the **bedrock** of healthy child development.*

• *Democracy is the **bedrock** of freedom.*

BELEAGUER
(be **leeg** ur)
Verb. To besiege. To annoy. To disturb. To surround with problems or annoyances. To trouble.

• *It seemed that every department **beleaguered** the CEO with personnel issues.*

• *The team was **beleaguered** with a series of critical injuries.*

BELLWETHER
(**bel weth** er)
Noun. A wether is a male sheep with a bell attached that leads a flock. By extension, the term bellwether has come to mean one whom others follow. One who takes the lead. Also, refers to lead indicators. An indication of current conditions and trends.

• *Certain stocks on the New York Stock Exchange are judged to be **bellwethers** of the overall condition of the market.*

*• The massive governmental report issued annually is considered by many to be a **bellwether** for economic trends.*

BENIGN
(be **nine**)

Adj. **The primary meaning is that which shows kindness. Showing gentleness, benevolence, and compassion. Pleasant or kindly.**

*• She loved those monthly visits to the country. Her grandmother's **benign** disposition and thoughtful and caring words were a constant source of inspiration.*

By extension, the word also means favorable, beneficial, or healthy. That which is helpful or constructive.

*• Because of its **benign** climate, the region attracted many of those afflicted with respiratory diseases.*

In pathology, it refers to that which has no significant effects, e.g., a benign tumor versus a malignant tumor.

BIANNUAL
Occurring twice a year.

BIENNIAL
Occurring every two years.

BIMONTHLY
Occurring every two months.

BIWEEKLY
Occurring every two weeks.

BIBLIOPHILE
(**bib** lee uh **file**)
Noun. A lover and collector of books.

BILL OF RIGHTS
The fundamental rights of the people as stated in the first ten Amendments of the Constitution.

BICAMERAL
(bi **kam** er ul)
Adj. Having two branches or chambers. By constitutional law the United States has a bicameral legislative system of government with assemblies consisting of the Senate and the House of Representatives. It is the same in Great Britain with the English Parliament divided into the British House of Lords and the British House of Commons. A unicameral system has only one legislative body. Nebraska is the only state in the Union to use a unicameral system of government.

BLANDISH
(**blan** dish)
Verb. To treat with flattery. To coax or cajole. To persuade with flattery. To persuade with gentle persistence. To convince by using flattery. To flatter sometimes dishonestly to gain an advantage. To adulate. Informally, to sweet talk.

• *In a very coquettish manner, the young girls attempted to **blandish** the doorman in to letting them pass through.*

• *For his personal aggrandizement, he has made a career of **blandishing** upper management.*

BLARNEY STONE

A stone in Ireland. It is believed by some that if you kiss this stone you become skilled at using flattery (blandishments).

BLITHE
(blithe)

Adj. **Carefree. Unconcerned. Lighthearted disposition. Easygoing. Apathetic or indifferent. Merry. Without worry.**

• *He is one of those rare individuals who seemingly go through life with a sense of **blithe** entitlement.*

• *We loved being around her. Her **blithe** spirit was contagious.*

• *What amazed us most was his **blithe** ignorance of the gravity of the situation.*

✪   The opposite of "blithe" is "solemn" or "somber."

BROMIDE
(**bro** mide)

> *Noun.* A chemical compound that typically includes only two elements, one of which is bromide. More commonly, the word has two other distinct meanings. One, a dull and unimaginative person. A person with conventional thoughts. Two, it is used to describe a commonplace, well-worn expression or saying. A hackneyed statement. A trite or obvious remark. A platitude. A statement used so much it has become meaningless.

> • *As they entered the locker room after losing the game because of a series of mistakes and mental errors, most on the team thought they would hear the same old coaching **bromides** like, "It's not if we won or lost, but how we played the game," etc., ad nauseam. But this time, the coach appeared totally frustrated, if not infuriated. "Gentlemen," he said, "it has been my experience in this world that there are three types of people: people who see things happen, people who make things happen, and people who wonder what happened! I believe most of you are in the last group!"*

B.T.U.

> British Thermal Unit. The amount of thermal energy required to raise the temperature of one pound of water one degree (F).

BUMPTIOUS
(**bump** shus)

> *Adj.* Offensively assertive. Arrogantly self-

assured. Conceited. Pushy or aggressive. Overly self-confident. Obtrusive.

• *His **bumptious** style oftentimes offends those around him.*

• *He was a cocky young rookie whose **bumptious** behavior did not sit well with the veterans on the team.*

Remember this word by associating that an encounter with such a person is similar to hitting a large "bump" in the road.

BY-AND-BY
The (near) future.

CAPACIOUS
(ca **pay** shus)
Adj. **Capable of holding much. Roomy. Large or spacious. Expansive.**

• *It was the most **capacious** room in the mansion.*

• *He had a **capacious** and facile mind that could take even the smallest idea and expand it into a much larger and more interesting view.*

CAPITAL
(**kap** uh tul)
Noun. A versatile word used to refer to those things generally categorized under the headings of: Government, Finance, Crime, and Grammar. Below are a few examples of how the word is used.

• *Capital–A city that is the center of government for a country, state, etc.*

• *Capital–Wealth in the form of property, securities, money, etc.*

• *Capital gains–Profits made by selling some asset.*

• *Capital gains tax–A tax levied on capital gains.*

• *Capital offense–A capital crime punishable by death.*

• *Capital letter–One of the upper case characters used as the first letter in the first word of a sentence or a proper name.*

• *Capital idea–Excellent or first-rate idea.*

AUTHOR'S NOTE
Capitol with an "o" is always a building. All other forms of the word use the letter "a."

CAPTIOUS
(**kap** shus)

Adj. **Faultfinding. Tending to express criticisms. Tending to find fault with the intent to quarrel. Hypercritical. Carping. One likely to notice trivial faults or defects. A propensity to stress faults and mistakes on the part of others. Censorious.**

• *Typically fueled by a few alcoholic drinks, she would from time to time launch into a **captious** diatribe,* *berating him for everything from his appearance to his career choices.*

• *Nothing is more annoying than to listen to a **captious** academic critic who, with no bestseller to his name, issues vitriolic assaults on recognized and widely acclaimed authors.*

• *The instructor at the management training session reminded those in attendance to avoid at all costs any **captious** statement regarding employee performance, particularly if made within earshot of others. He advised them on one of the cardinal rules of effective management:* **Praise in public–reprimand in private.**

CASTLES IN THE AIR
Visionary endeavors. Daydreams. Fanciful imaginations.

CELERITY
(suh **lare** uh tee)
Noun. **Quickness. Speed or swiftness. Rapidity of action or motion.**

• *The **celerity** with which he completed the project surprised everyone.*

• *It appears to many that the obsolescence of computer technology occurs with amazing **celerity**.*

• *The drill sergeant was amazed at the **celerity** with which the new recruits negotiated the obstacle course.*

CHIDE
(chide)

> *Verb.* **To scold. To find fault. To express disapproval. To carp. To reprimand. To admonish.**

> • *They were totally non-productive. They deserved to be **chided** for the inadequacy of their performance.*

> • *Never **chide** a young child without explaining why it is necessary.*

CHIRO-

> **Word element meaning "hand."**
> **The premise of chiropractic treatment is that normal conditions can be restored with adjustments made by hand to the spinal column.**

CIRCUMSPECT
(**sir** kum **spekt**)

> *Adj.* **Cautious. Prudent. Vigilant. Watchful. Reflective. Very attentive to the possible consequences of a particular action. Careful. Diligently viewed from all angles. Wary.**

> • *Because of the potential liability, we need to be more **circumspect** when terminating employees.*

> • *We are never more **circumspect** than when we know what we have written will come under the eye of a critical observer.*

AUTHOR'S NOTE
To remember this word, think of a (circ)le you might in(spect) from all angles.

CLANDESTINE
(klan **des** tin)

Adj. **Concealed. Conducted with secrecy. Withheld from public notice. Covert or undercover. Stealthy.**

• *He was charged with facilitating a **clandestine** method of passing government secrets to an agent of a foreign government.*

• *For over five years, the couple conducted a **clandestine** affair.*

COMITY
(**kom** uh tee)

Noun. **A state of harmony. Mutual respect between nations for the other's laws, customs, and political system (Comity of Nations). By extension it also means politeness. Civility. Courteousness. Graciousness.**

• *The President made an appeal for **comity** between the executive branch and Capitol Hill.*

• *The queen displayed the sort of **comity** one would expect from a person in her position.*

COMPENDIUM
(kum **pen** dee em)

Noun. **An extensive and comprehensive summary of a particular topic. An abridgement. An epitome. An abstract of a larger work.**

• *This manual is a **compendium** of $10 words.*

COMPLIMENT
(**com** pluh ment)

Noun/Verb. **As a noun it means an expression of praise. A tribute. An accolade. An admiring comment. An expression of esteem or respect. As a verb, it means to pay a compliment. To applaud or praise. To flatter.**

• *She received many* **compliments** *on her new hairstyle.*

• *He* **complimented** (verb form) *her on the efficient way she solved the problem.*

Do not confuse "compliment" with "complement." "Complement" is also both a noun and a verb. As a noun it means that which is added to a condition to make it complete or perfect. The quantity or number needed to make something whole. To remember the differences in these two words, think of the word "complete" which more closely resembles the word "complement."

• *To play golf well, you need a full* **complement** *of clubs.*

The above example implies the need for a "complete" set of clubs.

As a verb, the word "complement" means to supply that which is lacking. To supplement where a deficiency is implied. To round out. To augment or enrich.

• *The subdued and pastel colors of the wallpaper* **complemented** *the dark-stained, wooden paneling.*

COMPUNCTION
(kum **punk** shun)

> *Noun.* **Remorse. Regret. Self-reproach. Anxiety arising from guilt. Shame. Misgiving. Regret from some wrongdoing.**
>
> • *The convicted murderer showed no* **compunction** *for the crime he had committed.*
>
> • *She has received little job satisfaction from her time here. She indicated that she would have no* **compunction** *about quitting.*

CONCERTO
(kun **chair** tow)

> **A musical composition for one or more instruments with orchestral accompaniment. Typically performed in three movements, the concerto highlights the skill of the soloist. Johannes Brahams' Violin Concerto, OP.77 is an example.**

CONJECTURE
(kun **jek** chur)

> *Noun.* **An opinion formed without supporting evidence. Problematical. An inference made on the basis of insufficient evidence. Guesswork.**
>
> • *To attempt to explain his actions would only be* **conjecture** *on my part.*

• *Recently, there has been a great deal of **conjecture** issued by newspapers and business magazines on the likelihood of a woman being elected to the presidency of the United States.*

CONTIGUOUS
(kun **tig** u us)

Adj. **Touching or being side by side. Adjacent. In direct contact.**

• *The bank owns the land **contiguous** to ours.*

• *It is our desire to have an option to lease the office space **contiguous** to our existing space.*

Do not confuse this word with "continuous"(kun tin u us). **"Continuous" is an adjective that means unbroken, on-going, constant, or uninterrupted throughout space and time.**

• *The area was swamped with five days of **continuous** rain.*

This means it never stopped raining during that five-day period.

Keep in mind, however, that where "continuous" means unbroken, the adjective "continual" (kun tin u ul) describes something that stops from time to time, but continues over an extended period. Something repeated again and again. Persistent recurrence.

• *He has had **continual** problems with his cell phone since the day he purchased it.*

COPERNICUS

Polish astronomer (1473 - 1543) who first theorized that the earth and other planets revolve around the sun.

CORUSCATE
(**kor** uh **skate**)

Verb. To emit bright flashes of light. To sparkle. To gleam. To glitter.

• *As the plane banked into a turn for its final approach, she marveled at the sprawling lights of the city* **coruscating** *against the darkened sky.*

The word can also be used metaphorically to describe the brilliance of some object or thing.

• *The rich sounds of the music, which* **coruscated** *throughout the concert hall, mesmerized the audience.*

CROCODILE TEARS

False tears. It is fabled that crocodiles will shed tears over those they devour. Insincere. Disingenuous. Not honest.

CUM LAUDE
(kum **law** de)

(Latin) With honor. This Latin phrase is used to denote the third highest academic distinction or achievement.

• **Cum Laude**—*with honor.*

- *Magna **Cum Laude**–with great honor.*

- *Summa **Cum Laude**–with highest honor.*

- *He is a magna **cum laude** graduate.*

- *She graduated summa **cum laude**.*

DECIDUOUS
(duh **sij** u us)

Adj. **Describes trees and plants that shed their leaves at the end of the growing season, e.g., the red oak tree. Conversely, the live oak tree maintains it leaves year round.**

- *His one regret about the house he purchased twenty-five years ago was planting **deciduous** trees that yearly spread a blanket of leaves across his yard.*

DELETERIOUS
(**dell** uh **tier** e us)

Adj. **Harmful or injurious to your health.**

- *His **deleterious** lifestyle proved to be his undoing.*

- *After extensive testing, the new drug was found to have a **deleterious** effect on the central nervous system.*

✪ The opposite of "deleterious" is "salubrious," which means good for your health.

- *Convinced that the sea air would have a **salubrious** effect, she made plans for a two-week stay on the coast.*

DERISION
(duh **rizh** un)
> *Noun.* Ridicule or mockery. The use of scorn or ridicule to demonstrate contempt. Disrespect or disdain.
>
> • *Unfortunately for the new playwright, the play received considerable* **derision** *from the critics.*
>
> • *The* **derisive** (adjectival form) *actions and words occasionally directed at young children by other children can sometimes leave deep psychological scars that last a lifetime.*

DESCARTES, RENE
(day **kart**)
> French philosopher and mathematician who is credited with the now famous quote, *"Cogito ergo sum."* It means, "I think therefore I am."

DESULTORY
(**des** ul **tor** e)
> *Adj.* Moving about from one thing to another. Not methodical. Without a clear plan. Random. Haphazard or aimless. Hit and miss. Disconnected.
>
> • *Typical of most cocktail parties is the* **desultory** *nature of the conversations.*
>
> • *He refused to arduously apply himself and gave only* **desultory** *efforts to the assignment that had been given him.*

45

• *To eliminate the* **desultory** *manner in which he handled his responsibilities, he was asked to prepare a "to do" list every day.*

✪   The opposite of "desultory" is "methodical" or "deliberate."

DIDACTIC
(die **dak** tik)

> *Adj.* **Instructive. Designed to teach. Conveying instruction. Edifying and informative. Educational. The word is also used to indicate that which is overly instructive. Showing a tendency to give advice or instruction even if it is not requested or wanted. Showing a tendency to moralize or preach.**

> • *The Bible is* **didactic** *since it provides guidance on moral and ethical behavior.*

> • *The essay was a* **didactic** *account of the history of Gothic architecture.*

> • *She became irritated when at times on the golf course his instructions about the golf swing became too* **didactic.**

The noun "didactics" refers to the art or science of teaching.

DIERESIS
(die **err** uh sis)

> **The ¨ sign placed over the top of the second of**

two adjacent vowels to indicate a separate pronunciation.

• *Coöperate would be pronounced "coup erate" without
the **dieresis** over the second "o."*

DIFFIDENT
(**diff** uh dent)
> *Adj.* Timid. Lacking in confidence. Faint-hearted.
> In doubt of one's own ability. Lacking self-assur-
> ance. Insecure. Shy or apprehensive.

> • *One of the negative effects of overbearing parents is
> the possibility of raising **diffident** children.*

> • *Despite the successes that highlighted his business
> career, he remained **diffident** about his accomplish-
> ments.*

> • *Meeting women never came easily for him. As she
> approached, he sensed those familiar, **diffident** feelings
> beginning to well within him.*

✪   The opposite of "diffident" is "brash."

DILATORY
(**dill** uh **tor** e)
> *Adj.* Causing or intending to delay. Procrastinat-
> ing. Deferring.

> • *His **dilatory** efforts will cause us to miss the dead-
> line.*

• *Congress has been* **dilatory** *in passing effective legis-lation that protects the environment.*

Also, a dilatory strategy is one intentionally designed to prolong matters for the purpose of gaining time or delaying action.

• *Their request for additional documentation appears to be a* **dilatory** *effort to preclude action on our part.*

DISCORD
(**dis** cord)

Noun. **Absence of harmony between persons or things. Disagreement. At variance. At odds. Lack of agreement.**

• *The two groups were in* **discord** *on the most efficient method of completing the task.*

• *The couple's marital* **discord** *affected his performance on the job.*

The adjectival form of "discord" is "discordant" (dis **kor** dunt).

• *It was an overnight best seller. At the time, however, the contemporary dialogue employed by Jack Kerouac in his 1957 novel,* On The Road, *struck a* **discordant** *note for many readers.*

> **AUTHOR'S NOTE**
> Kerouac is credited with coining the phrase, "The Beat Generation," a social and literary movement of the 1950s, and was one of its most prominent members. Interestingly, he did not prepare the text for *On The Road* on single sheets of paper. It was typed on one long scroll of teletype paper, and in 2001 the scroll was purchased by Jim Irsay, the owner of the Indianapolis Colts, for $2.4 million dollars.

DISCREET
(dis **kreet**)

Adj. **Cautious. Judicious. Prudent. Careful.**

• *A discreet investor will analyze all aspects of a corporation including its management team, products, market share, and profits.*

• *Since company officials were interested in having him join their management team, they made **discreet** inquiries into his background.*

Do not confuse this word with the adjective "discrete" (pronounced the same way as "discreet"), which means detached, separate, or distinct.

• *It is a large holding company with each of its companies operating as **discrete** entities.*

DISIMPASSIONED
(dis em **pash** und)

> *Adj.* Calm. Passionless. Without emotion. Composed and unruffled. Indifferent or detached. Impartial. Collected.

> • *He explained our options with a **disimpassioned** look on his face.*

> • *During an employee performance evaluation, the manager must express his opinions and observations in a fair and **disimpassioned** manner.*

> • *She gave a lively and spirited speech full of humor and personal anecdotes that was certainly a change of pace from previous **disimpassioned** university lecturers.*

✪   The opposite of "disimpassioned" is "emotional."

Do not confuse "disimpassioned" with the adjective "dispassionate." "Dispassionate" means not influenced by emotions or personal feelings. Unbiased. Objective. Not influenced by prejudice. Impartial.

> • *Amid the chaos and hysteria that blanketed the city, he nonetheless provided a **dispassionate** analysis of the events that had transpired.*

DISINGENUOUS
(dis in **jen** u us)

> *Adj.* **Lacking in frankness, candor, or sincerity. Not honest or forthright. Guileful and deceitful. Not completely truthful. Not ingenuous.**
>
> • *His skeptical remarks concerning the potential value of the painting seem* **disingenuous** *when you consider he is a highly acclaimed art critic.*
>
> • *It is* **disingenuous** *of him to claim that his poor performance resulted from lack of direction and poor management.*

DISINTERESTED
(dis **in** tuh **res** tid)

> *Adj.* **Impartial. Unbiased. Not influenced by self-interests. Fair and open minded. With no stake in the outcome. Objective. Without prejudice.**
>
> • *The two opposing sides agreed that a* **disinterested** *third party was needed to mediate their dispute.*
>
> **"Disinterested" does *not* mean "uninterested," and the words should not be used interchangeably. "Uninterested" means lacking in interest or having no interest. Indifferent. Unconcerned.**
>
> • *She was totally* **uninterested** *in their dispute, but agreed that a disinterested third party was needed.*

DUPLICITY
(du **pliss** uh tee)

> *Noun.* **Double dealing. Saying different things to two different parties. Talking or acting in two dissimilar ways concerning the same matter. Covering up one's true intention by misleading statements and actions. That which is deceptive. Dishonest. Acting in bad faith. Fraudulence.**

> • *The real estate commission revoked his license because of his **duplicity**. He was hired by a client to find an office building for sale, then reported back that none were available at a good price. Subsequently, he purchased for his own account a building that was priced below market that he discovered during his search.*

> • *The newspaper published a scathing account of the **duplicitous** (**adjectival form**) actions of the city manager.*

EFFICACY
(**eff** uh kuh see)

> *Noun.* **The capacity for producing desired results. The ability to achieve what is planned. The ability to achieve an expected outcome.**

> • *With so few resources being brought to bear, he questioned the **efficacy** of the plan.*

> • *The **efficacy** of any sales training program can be measured by the volume of resulting sales.*

EGREGIOUS
(e **gree** jus)

Adj. **Remarkably flagrant. Glaring. Conspicuously bad. Blatantly outrageous. Reprehensible. Clearly disgraceful.**

• *It was an* ***egregious*** *error for the ambassador to mispronounce the prime minister's name.*

• *The sales team was advised not to commit the most* ***egregious*** *mistake of all:* ***underestimating your competitor's ability to perform while overestimating your own.***

• *The heart will tell you that it is a grossly* ***egregious*** *injustice for a small child to be afflicted with a terminal illness.*

EMBLEMATIC
(**em** bluh **mat** ik)

Adj. **Pertaining to an emblem. It also refers to that which is symbolic of or representative of the nature of people, places, or ideas. Typifies.**

• *Her actions of faith and charity are* ***emblematic*** *of her religious background.*

• *His reluctance to participate actively in the training exercises is* ***emblematic*** *of his lack of dedication.*

.

EMERALD ISLE
Ireland.

GARDEN ISLAND
Kauai, Hawaii.

EMINENT DOMAIN
The right of a governmental agency to take possession of private property for public use with fair compensation paid to the owner. Usually for streets, right of ways, parks, etc.

ENGENDER
(in **jen** der)
Verb. To bring about or make happen. To give rise to. To cause to exist. To spawn.

• *Hatred* **engenders** *violence.*

• *Her willingness to actively support his cause* **engendered** *a strong bond of friendship between them.*

ENIGMA
(uh **nig** muh)
Noun. Something difficult to comprehend. Inexplicable. Not easily understood. A puzzle. Something difficult to explain. Mysterious. Something that baffles understanding.

• *His disappearance was an* **enigma** *to police officials.*

• *Because of the unusual and abnormal way he lived his life, he was described as an* **enigmatic** (**adjectival**

form) *young man who grew into an enigmatic old man.*

• *By design or otherwise, Leonardo da Vinci has had the world marveling for centuries at the famously* **enigmatic** *smile on the face of the Mona Lisa.*

The word can be used to describe people, places, or things.

ENJOIN
(en **join**)

Verb. **The primary meaning of "enjoin" is to command or to direct. To charge with a duty. To impose with authority. To require an action. To order something done.**

• *The vice president of personnel* **enjoined** *the field managers to prepare performance evaluations for each of their direct reports.*

• *While touring the plant facilities, the manager of New Product Development* **enjoined** *us to keep all information confidential.*

The secondary meaning of "enjoin" is to prohibit or to forbid. To restrain as with an injunction. To prevent. To inhibit.

• *She was* **enjoined** *by her own conscience from participating in such questionable activity.*

> ### AUTHOR'S NOTE
> This is a very interesting word in that the primary meaning of the word is to be charged with doing something; the secondary meaning is to be charged with *not* doing something. Thus, "enjoin" is one of just a few words in the English language that is its own antonym. The opposite of "enjoin" is "enjoin."

EPHEMERAL
(e **fem** uh rul)
> *Adj.* **Lasting a short time. Fleeting. Transient.**

> • *Fame is sometimes **ephemeral**. One only needs to allude to the careers of "one-hit wonder" rock groups to understand the meaning of **ephemeral**.*

> • *While others might judge their two-day relationship to have been **ephemeral**, it left a lasting impression on his mind.*

> • *To achieve contentment in the course of your life, you must be able to separate those things that are **ephemeral** from those of lasting value.*

EPICURE
(**epp** uh **cure**)
> *Noun.* **A person who has developed a refined taste in eating and drinking.**

> • *He enjoyed immensely the sensual pleasure of dining*

*in the most elegant restaurants in Western Europe and quickly became known as a world traveler and **epicure**.*

Do not confuse this word with its adjectival form "epicurean." "Epicurean" is the adjective used to describe the habits, tastes, and characteristics of an "epicure."

EPIGRAM
(**epp** uh **gram**)

Noun. **Any clever or pointed saying concisely expressed.**

• *The following **epigram** clearly expresses our feelings toward loud, empty-headed individuals: "The empty drum makes the most noise."*

ELEGY
(**el** uh gee)

Noun. **A poem that expresses sorrow. A lament. A mournful, plaintive poem. An example is** *Elegy Written in a Country Churchyard* **by Thomas Gray (1716–1771).**

EULOGY
(**you** luh gee)

Noun. **A speech or talk of praise for a person who has died.**

EPITAPH
(**epp** uh **taff**)

>*Noun.* **An inscription engraved in the tombstone or monument of a person who has died.**
>
>• *"Here lies John Brown*
>*Beloved husband*
>*And caring father."*
>
>**Others have been inscribed less eloquently.**
>
>• *"Here lies Les Moore*
>*Shot in the head with a .44*
>*No less. No more."*
>
>• *"Here lies my wife*
>*Here let her lie*
>*She's finally at rest*
>*And so am I."*
>
>• *"I told you I wasn't*
>*feeling very well."*

EPITHET
(**epp** uh **thet**)

>**A term or expression applied to a person to indicate a significant accomplishment or characteristic.**
>
>• *Alexander, The Great.*
>
>• *Ronald Reagan, The Great Communicator.*

It is also used to indicate some criticism or some negative characteristic.

• *A departmental manager—"The All-knowing One."*

• *An overweight opera singer—"The Two-Ton Tenor."*

EQUINOX
(e kwuh **noks**)

Noun. Literally translated the word means "equal night" in reference to the two times a year when day and night are of equal length. It occurs in the Northern Hemisphere around March 20th and is called the Vernal Equinox. It occurs again in the fall around September 22nd and is called the Autumnal Equinox. It is at these two points in time that the sun crosses directly over the plane of the earth's equator, making daytime and nighttime of equal length.

AUTHOR'S NOTE

There is a persistent notion that because of some strange gravitational force occurring on these two days, one can easily balance an egg on its end. However, there is no change in gravitational force. If you have the time and the patience, you can balance an egg on its end anytime of the year. For those of you with little patience, or for those of you who just want to impress your friends, sprinkle a few grains of salt on a flat surface. Balance the egg, and when your friends are not looking, blow the excess salt away.

EQUIVOCAL
(e **kwiv** uh cul)

Adj. **Of questionable meaning. Not clearly understood. Nebulous. Vague. Oftentimes used with intent to deceive. If not, it is just ambiguous.**

• *Since the recommendations were subject to different interpretations, the group deemed the report too* ***equivocal.***

• *He gave an* ***equivocal*** *statement to the press, neither denying nor confirming the allegations.*

Something unequivocal is clearly and easily understood.

• *Her instructions to the class were brief and* ***unequivocal.***

ERUDITE
(**err** uh **dite**)

Adj. **Scholarly or learned. Having profound knowledge. Well-educated. Cultured.**

• *An* ***erudite*** *professor.*

• *It is hard to imagine a more* ***erudite*** *group of individuals.*

"Erudition" is acquired knowledge through extensive study.

EUPHEMISM
(**u** fuh **miz** em)
> *Noun.* **The substitution of a bland, indirect or non-specific statement for a harsh one.**
>
> • *"He passed away" is a* **euphemism** *for "he died."*
>
> • *"Adult films" is a* **euphemism** *for "pornographic movies."*
>
> • *In the corporate world, "downsizing" is a* **euphemism** *for "firings" and "layoffs."*

EXACERBATE
(ig **zas** er bate)
> *Verb.* **To make something already bad even worse. To worsen. To aggravate. To inflame or make more severe. To intensify a condition. To irritate a condition.**
>
> • *He was not a popular political figure and his entry into the election only served to* **exacerbate** *the ethnic tensions within the country.*
>
> • *Rising fuel costs* **exacerbated** *the small airline's ability to return to profitability.*
>
> • *The President's statement to the press* **exacerbated** *the political strain between the White House and Congress.*
>
> ✪   The opposite of "exacerbate" is "improve."

EXIGENT
(**ek** suh gent)

> *Adj.* Urgent. Requiring quick action. Pressing. Needing immediate attention. Imperative. Critical.

> • *The lack of food and supplies for the front line troops was an **exigent** problem for the logistics group.*

> • *The company was forced to seek additional lines of credit because of its **exigent** financial condition.*

EXPUNGE
(ik **spunj**)

> *Verb.* To remove or blot out. To erase. Usually refers to inanimate objects such as words, ideas, or notions.

> • *Most established authors take great exception to editors who attempt to **expunge** passages from their submitted drafts.*

> • *On the first day of class, the wise old professor set out to **expunge** the notion that the use of $25 words in the students' writing exercises would make them appear intellectually superior.*

FASCISM
(**fash** ism)

> A governmental system emphasizing strong central control by a dictator over all matters of state. Established in Italy in 1922 by Benito Mussolini, it imparted strong influence on the Nazi Party

in Germany. At the heart of the movement was contempt for democracy and the belief in a strong demagogic approach. The movement lost influence after 1945, but existed in Spain and Portugal until the mid-1970s.

FATHOM
(**fath** em)

Noun/Verb. **In nautical terms, a unit of measurement equal to six (6) feet in depth. The word is derived from the Old English word "faethm," which means outstretched arms, and is the original definition of the measurement.**

As a verb, it means to fully understand something. To understand or grasp the meaning of. To perceive with the senses or get to the bottom of it.

*• It is difficult to **fathom** why "reality" television shows achieve such high ratings.*

*• It is almost impossible to **fathom** the logic behind his actions.*

FECKLESS
(**fek** lis)

Adj. **Useless. Ineffective. Having no worth. Fruitless. Unproductive or futile.**

*• You set in motion what now appears to be a **feckless** approach to resolving the crisis.*

• *He took exception to the implication that he was a* **feckless** *drunk; he simply saw himself as a man with minimal expectations who liked to take a drink or two.*

• *Many* **feckless** *attempts have been made to improve the diplomatic relations between India and Pakistan.*

FLIPPANT
(**flip** ent)

Adj. **Glib. Facetious. Bringing disrespectful humor to bear on a serious matter. Disrespectful levity.**

• *His* **flippant** *reply to the question of why his grade point average was so low was an indication to the advisor that the student had little or no desire to apply himself.*

• *What we need is a serious discussion. What we don't need is unrestrained* **flippancy** (noun form).

FORGO
(for **go**)

Verb. **To give up. To relinquish or do without. To let go by or to abandon.**

• *We should* **forgo** *the preliminaries and get right to the heart of the matter.*

• *In order to complete the project on time, we had to* **forgo** *lunch.*

A variant form of "forgo" is "forego" and is pronounced the same. It is a verb meaning to precede. To have happened before or to go before. To have occurred earlier in time. It is a verb used most often as a present or past participle.

• *The foregoing* (present participle) *advertisement was a paid political announcement.*

• *As the returns came in, the result of the election seemed to be a foregone* (past participle) *conclusion.*

FORTHRIGHT
(forth right)

Adj. Going straight to the heart of a matter. Direct. Straightforward. Up-front and candid.

• *The presiding judge reminded the witness that he should provide only forthright and concise answers and to avoid additional comments.*

• *You have to admire the forthright manner in which she deals with these problems.*

FORTHWITH
(forth with)

Adv. Without delay. At once. Immediately. Instantly. Promptly.

• *You are hereby advised to provide this information forthwith.*

• *If he is proven to be guilty, he should be relieved forthwith of his responsibilities.*

FORTNIGHT

A contraction of two words from Middle English meaning fourteen nights. A period of time equaling fourteen days and nights. Two weeks.

FORTUITOUS

(for **too** uh tus)

Adj. Unanticipated. Accidental. Occurring by chance. Unforeseen. It does *not* mean fortunate or lucky.

• *While traveling to separate cities, the two ex-lovers had a fortuitous encounter at the airport.*

"Fortuitous" simply means unplanned or accidental. A fortuitous meeting at the airport could have good or bad consequences. There is widespread use of the word to indicate good fortune, probably because it resembles the word "fortunate." However, prescriptive grammarians agree that the word is being misused in that context. Use the word only to mean occurring by chance or accidental.

Good fortune discovered accidentally is "serendipitous."

FOURSCORE

A word made famous by Abraham Lincoln. Four (4) x score (20) = 80. The first five words of his 1863 Gettysburg Address, "Fourscore and seven years ago" is a reference to the eighty-seven years that had passed since the signing of the Declaration of Independence (1776).

FOURTH ESTATE

A collective term referring to newspapers, reporters, and news journalists. The national press corps.

FRUGAL
(**fru** gul)

Adj. A trait among those individuals who save prudently and spend sparingly. Thrifty. Parsimonious.

• *"Mom says Uncle Bill is just being **frugal**. Dad says he's tight as a tick."*

• *He was a wealthy man with simple and **frugal** tastes.*

A characteristic opposite that of a spendthrift.

FURLONG
(**fur** long)

A unit of measurement equaling 220 yards or 1/8th of a mile.

FURTIVE
(**fur** tive)

Adj. Secretive. Stealthy. Shifty. Clandestine or surreptitious. Willfully avoiding observation or recognition. Sneaky.

• *He had a **furtive** look about him that made us doubt the validity of his accusations.*

• *Their **furtive** efforts to elude capture were in vain.*

GALVANIC
(gal **van** ik)

Adj. In electrical engineering, it pertains to electricity that is produced by the chemical action of two dissimilar metals with other liquids, e.g., a car battery. More commonly, the word is used to describe that which produces an electric effect. Shocking. Intensely exciting. Stimulating. Energizing. That which inspires or motivates. Electrifying.

• *The new regional vice president had a **galvanic** effect on the morale of the employees in his region.*

• *Everyone in the room felt her **galvanic** presence.*

• *His stirring speech **galvanized** (**verb form**) the group into taking immediate action.*

AUTHOR'S NOTE
This word entered the English language as a result of Luigi Galvani (1737–1798), an Italian physiologist whose early experiments eventually led to the discovery that chemical action can generate electricity.

GARRULOUS
(**gare** uh lus)

Adj. Talkative. Verbose. Given to much talk about insignificant matters. Loquacious.

• *Being **garrulous** was one of the unique and more*

amusing characteristics of the old man. He could ramble on for hours as long as someone would listen.

• *It was a rambling and **garrulous** speech that indicated he had spent little time in its preparation.*

GENEVA CONVENTION

An international agreement among nations that outlines a set of rules for the proper and humane treatment of those who have been wounded or captured.

GEORGE ELIOT

A pseudonym for a British novelist whose real name was Mary Ann Evans (1819–1880), author of the novel *Silas Marner*. It was written in 1861 and attempted to demonstrate that the love of those around us is ultimately more rewarding than the love of money.

GERMANE
(jer **main**)

Adj. Related or relevant. That which is pertinent. That which is applicable. That which is connected with or significant to what is being done or discussed.

• *His comments were not **germane** to the topic of our discussion.*

• *Her questions are **germane** to the issues. His questions could not have been less relevant.*

✪   The opposite of "germane" is "unconnected."

GERUND
(**jer** end)

Noun. A noun derived from verbs by adding *–ing* with the resulting word being used as the subject, the direct object, or the object of a preposition in a sentence.

The words "write" and "run" are verbs. By adding *–ing,* the verbs are converted to gerunds.

• **Writing** *is sometimes difficult.*

• **Running** *is good exercise.*

In these examples, "writing" and "running" are gerunds and are the subjects of the sentences.

As stated in the definition, gerunds also function as direct objects and objects of prepositions

• *She enjoys* **reading** (direct object).

• *These ingredients are used for* **baking** (object of preposition).

G. I.

A colloquial expression for an enlisted person in the U. S. Army. (G)overnment (I)ssue.

GOLDEN GATE

A strait is a narrow passage of water that connects two larger bodies of water. The Golden Gate Strait connects the Pacific Ocean with San

Francisco Bay. The Golden Gate Bridge spans the strait. The main span portion of the suspended structure measures 4,200 feet. The total length of the bridge, including approaches, measures 8,981 feet. The width of the bridge is 90 feet.

GOLF LINKS
A golf course. The name is derived from a Scottish reference to building a golf course on land unsuitable to vegetative growth that lies between the ocean and fertile soil. Hence, it was referred to as a link between the ocean and the productive land.

GRAND COULEE
The Grand Coulee Dam is located on the Columbia River in central Washington and is made from 12 million cubic yards of concrete. As such, it is the largest concrete structure in the United States.

GREAT BRITAIN
An island northwest of the European mainland that includes the countries of England, Scotland, and Wales.

The term United Kingdom refers to the three countries of Great Britain plus Northern Ireland.

GREAT LAKES
A series of five lakes located between the United States and Canada. Remember their names with

this acronym–H.O.M.E.S. Huron, Ontario, Michigan, Erie, and Superior.

Lake Superior is not only the largest of the Great Lakes, but it is the largest freshwater lake in the world by surface area. It covers approximately 31,700 square miles.

GREELEY, HORACE

A U. S. politician and journalist (1811–1872). He launched the *New York Tribune* and was one of the founders of the Republican Party. He advised American youth to "Go west young man and grow with the country."

GREENWICH MEAN TIME

GMT, also called Coordinated Universal Time (UTC), is international time and the basis for the world time clock. The acronym UTC was adopted by the International Telecommunications Union as a compromise between those who wanted the English form of CUT and those who advocated the French form of TUC (*temps universel coordonne*). Zulu Time is an aviation and military expression for UTC and virtually means the same thing. The Greenwich meridian or prime meridian (longitude zero degrees) passes through the Royal Observatory in Greenwich, England, and is the starting point of every time zone in the world. There are twenty-five World Time Zones with integers ranging from–12 to 0 (GMT) and from 0 (GMT) to +12. Each zone is 15 degrees of longitude as measured East to West from the

Prime Meridian. For example, Central Standard Time (CST) is designated−6. This means that if the GMT were 7:00 p.m., the Central Standard Time would be 1:00 p.m.

HAPLESS
(**hap** lis)

> *Adj.* **Most think this word means "helpless." It does not. It means without luck. Unfortunate. Unlucky. Untoward or inopportune.**
>
> • *He found himself a* **hapless** *victim of an improbable and unlikely set of circumstances.*
>
> • *Children are oftentimes the* **hapless** *casualties of broken homes.*

HAUGHTY
(**haw** tee)

> *Adj.* **Overly proud. Arrogant. Disdainful. A high opinion of one's self. Supercilious. Convinced of one's own superiority or importance.**
>
> • *While no one could deny the success she had attained, you had to wonder if that success justified her oftentimes* **haughty** *behavior.*
>
> • *Eventually, his* **haughty** *mannerisms and feelings of self-importance will derail his ability to effectively manage people.*

HIGH SEAS

International waters. Seas and oceans outside of the three-mile limit of a country's coastline. Inside the three-mile limit is referred to as inland waters.

HOMONYM

(**hom** uh nim)

Noun. A word that sounds like another word but has a different meaning.

• *"Bear" and "bare" or "meat" and "meet."*

> **AUTHOR'S NOTE**
> A university English professor relates that a number of her students have turned in essays that included the phrase, "the right to bare arms." She instructs her students that she seriously doubts the founding fathers were concerned over their constitutional right to get a sun tan.

HORSEPOWER

A unit of power. The rate at which work is done. The concept of horsepower was first introduced by James Watt (1736–1819), a Scottish engineer and inventor. One horsepower equals 33,000 foot-pounds of work per minute or the power necessary to lift 33,000 pounds a distance of one foot in one minute. The name "horsepower" was coined since actual horses were used in the experiments. The watt as a unit of power is named after James Watt. The electrical equivalent of one horsepower is 746 watts.

HOUSE OF COMMONS

The House of Commons is a component of the Parliament of the United Kingdom and is by far the dominant branch. Its 659 members are elected to office by the people.

HOUSE OF LORDS

The House of Lords is a component of the Parliament of the United Kingdom. Its members are non-elected. In addition to legislative activity, the House of Lords has certain judicial responsibilities. Members of this assembly who have legal experience act as the highest court of appeals in the United Kingdom. The House of Lords consists of 26 members who are clerics of the Church of England and 669 members from the Peerage. The Peerage consists of those who hold titles of nobility and those who have received awards and decorations bestowed by the Sovereign.

HYPER-

A prefix meaning "over" or above that which is normal.

• *Hypertension is a condition of elevated blood pressure within the human body.*

HYPO-
A prefix meaning "under" or below that which is normal.

• *Hypothermia is a condition in which the temperature of the body is lower than normal.*

Think of the "o" in low to remember the difference between these two prefixes.

HYPERBOLE
(hi **purr** buh lee)
Noun. **An exaggerated statement to achieve a desired effect. Obviously overstated. Not intended to be literal.**

• *It is better to avoid **hyperbole**. Not one writer in 20 million can use it correctly.*

• *"I have told you a million, billion times, don't exaggerate!"*

IDIOM
(**id** e em)
Noun. **Expressions peculiar to a language. A group of words in a sentence that has a meaning or connotation different from what the words actually express. Sometimes a form or variation of a language.**

• *One of the more compelling facts about the life of Danish writer Hans Christian Andersen (1805–1875) was his decision to separate himself from liter-*

*ary tradition and write interesting and imaginative stories with the **idioms** and constructions of the spoken language.*

• *The following are a few examples of **idioms** in use today:*

  • *A bull in a china shop.*

  • *No bed of roses.*

  • *It's raining cats and dogs.*

  • *A rule of thumb.*

Notice that while the words in the above sentences say one thing, the phrase has an entirely different connotation.

IGNOMINIOUS
(**ig** nuh **men** e us)

> *Adj.* **Shameful. Disgraceful. Dishonorable. Inglorious. That which could engender public contempt.**

• *To have lost the Super Bowl by a score of 42–0 can only be described as an **ignominious** defeat.*

• *President Richard M. Nixon **ignominiously** (**adverbial form**) resigned his presidency at the height of the Watergate scandal.*

ILL-ADVISED
(**il**-ad **vized**)

Adj. **Something done without prudent study or consideration. Not totally analyzed.**

• *It is an **ill-advised** plan that would bring a product to market without a comprehensive demographic analysis.*

• *There are some who consider the preemptive strike against Iraq by the United States to have been an **ill-advised** endeavor.*

ILLUSTRIOUS
(il **lus** tree us)

Adj. **Renowned. Prominent. Highly distinguished. Notable. Well respected. Highly admired.**

• *She is now at the end of a long and **illustrious** career.*

• *He comes from an **illustrious** political family whose members have held numerous governmental positions both locally and nationally.*

INTERDICT
(**in** ter **dickt**)

Verb. **To forbid by decree. To stop. To prohibit. To disallow or to bar.**

• *Increased security has been put in place along the border in an attempt to **interdict** drug smuggling activity.*

• *During the Cuban missile crisis, President Kennedy ordered the U. S. Navy to establish a blockade that would* **interdict** *Russian ships steaming toward Cuba.*

• *According to some historians, President Kennedy's decision to issue an* **interdiction** **(noun form)** *of Russian ships was one of the most daunting decisions ever made by an American president.*

IMMINENT
(**em** uh nent)

> *Adj.* **Something about to happen. Impending. Looming in the near future. The word implies an ominous or threatening event.**

> • *With the Russian ships steaming toward the block-ade, most Americans believed war was* **imminent***.*

> **Be careful not to confuse "imminent" with the adjective "eminent" (em** uh nent**). "Eminent" means standing above others. Prominent. High in rank or reputation. Distinguished. Well-known. Respected and renowned. Celebrated.**

> • *An* **eminent** *physician.*

> • *She was an* **eminent** *psychologist who gained national acclaim for her scientific research in the field of artificial intelligence.*

IMMODERATE
(em **mod** er it)

> *Adj.* **More than is necessary. Exorbitant. Goes**

beyond reasonable limits. Excessive. Remember that it always implies more and not less than what would be considered moderate.

• *There are a number of shareholders who believe the current management group is guilty of **immoderate** spending.*

• *They have spent an **immoderate** amount of time completing a project that should have taken only a few hours.*

IMMUTABLE
(em **mu** tuh bul)
> *Adj.* **Not capable of being changed. Unalterable. Unchallengeable. That which cannot be assailed. A condition "cast in stone."**

• *His mind was made up. He remained **immutable** on the subject.*

• *While she was not a fanatically religious person, she did have **immutable** faith that a Divine power was guiding her actions.*

IMPERIOUS
(em **peer** e us)
> *Adj.* **Dictatorial. High-handed and overbearing. Domineering. Over-controlling.**

• *His **imperious** approach to managing a sales team will not last the test of time.*

*• He was a gifted and skilled surgeon, but the staff in the emergency room intensely disliked his **imperious** attitude.*

IMPERVIOUS

(em **purr** vee us)

> *Adj.* **That which is not penetrable. Impermeable. Fully resistant. Not influenced. Not affected.**
>
> *• It seemed as though his mind was **impervious** to the logical arguments being presented.*
>
> *• It appears to be a trait among U. S. politicians that they remain **impervious** to the criticisms of both the press and members of the opposing political party.*

AUTHOR'S NOTE

Some of Ronald Reagan's political opponents felt that he was seemingly impervious to criticism since nothing disreputable ever stuck to his reputation. Hence, he was humorously referred to as "The Teflon President."

IMPERTINENT

(em **purr** tuh nent)

> *Adj.* **Improperly forward or bold. Insolent. Impudent. Implies rude and disrespectable behavior. Impolite. Exceeding the boundaries of proper behavior. Discourteous.**
>
> *• She was shocked that someone would make such an **impertinent** remark during such a solemn occasion.*

• **(An actual occurrence at the branch office of a major computer manufacturer.)** *The sales manager was visibly irritated by the salesperson's **impertinent** reply. During a training session, the manager was attempting to make a point about the need to increase sales performance. He asked, "Do any of you know what happens around here to salesmen who can't sell?" From the back of the room he heard, "Yeah, they make you a manager!"*

The word also means that which does not pertain to what is being considered or discussed. Not pertinent. Not relevant. Not applicable. That which has no bearing on the topic at hand.

• *Unfortunately, he wasted everyone's time by bringing up several **impertinent** facts before he got to the matter under consideration.*

IMPETUOUS
(em **pech** u us)

Adj. **Impulsive. Sudden actions without the benefit of forethought. Rash. Hasty. Overly eager.**

• *She was young and **impetuous** and cradled a burning desire to take Hollywood by storm.*

• *The **impetuous** secretary took matters into her own hands.*

• *He made a fatal error in his presentation when he moved **impetuously** (**adverbial form**) to a recommended solution before the customer fully realized the extent of the problem that needed solving.*

IMPLICIT
(em **plis** it)

>*Adj.* **Not expressly stated. Understood without being said. Inherent. An existing condition even though it is not obvious or apparent.**

>• *By not replying to the question, his consent was* ***implicit***.

>• *It was* ***implicit*** *in his actions that he was not totally committed to the recommendations we had made.*

IMPROVIDENT
(em **prov** uh dent)

>*Adj.* **Neglecting future requirements or needs. Imprudent. Incautious. Exhibiting a lack of forethought.**

>• *It would seem* ***improvident*** *at best to start a family with no visible means of support.*

>• *Their* ***improvident*** *decisions led them into bankruptcy.*

AUTHOR'S NOTE
Benjamin Franklin supplied the most insightful quote issued on improvidence. He said, "By failing to prepare, you are preparing to fail."

IMPUGN
(em **pune**)

> *Verb.* **To challenge by words another's character or veracity. To call into question an individual's actions, motives, or honesty.**

> • *I will not have you **impugn** my character with such questions.*

> • *The U. S. presidential debates do not appear to be real debates at all. Rather, they seem to be a series of alternating statements made by each candidate **impugning** the competency of the other.*

INADVERTENT
(en add **vur** tent)

> *Adj.* **Accidental. Unplanned and unintended. Not deliberate. Also means characterized by lack of attentiveness.**

> • *Leaving her name off of the invitation list was an **inadvertent** mistake.*

> • *He **inadvertently** (**adverbial form**) forgot to insert the drawings in the presentation material.*

INANE
(en **ane**)

> *Adj.* **Lacking sense or logic. Empty or void of substance. Absurd. Illogical. Mindless.**

> • *The group ridiculed him for his **inane** remarks.*

• *His **inane** attempts to cover up the mistakes he had made were remarkably illogical and only served to exacerbate the problem.*

INAPPREHENSIBLE
(**en** app ree **hen** suh bul)

Adj. **That which cannot be grasped by the senses or understood by the intellect. Unclear. Unintelligible. Not understandable.**

• *The kindest thing one can say about the drug-induced teachings of this religious fanatic is that mostly they are **inapprehensible**.*

Do not confuse this word with "inapprehensive." "Inapprehensive" is the negative form of "apprehensive," which means to be wary of some impending event that may or may not happen in the future.

The word "incomprehensible" has a similar meaning to "inapprehensible." It means not comprehensible or not understandable.

INCIPIENT
(en **sip** e ent)

Adj. **Just beginning. Budding. Embryonic. In an initial stage or just starting to appear.**

• *With only a few members included within its ranks, the new political movement was clearly in an **incipient** state of development.*

• *The newspaper article marked* **incipient** *public concern over rerouting a portion of the freeway.*

INSIPID
(en **sip** id)

   Adj. **When used to describe a speech, conversation, or the like, it means dull and uninteresting. Colorless or unexciting. When used to describe food it means tasteless, bland, or flavorless.**

   • *It was an* **insipid** *speech that had most of the audience slouching in their chairs and longing to hear the phrase, "And finally. . . ."*

   • *She didn't know which was worse: the injury or the* **insipid** *hospital food.*

INCONGRUOUS
(en **cong** grew us)

   Adj. **Inconsistent with established conditions. Out of place. Incompatible. Not associating harmoniously.**

   • *These are actions* **incongruous** *with company standards.*

   • *How* **incongruous** *and irrational it is for a known adulterer to be moralizing on the merits of Christian values.*

   • *They made an* **incongruous** *pair: he was short and she was tall; she was loud and garrulous while he was quiet and reserved.*

INCULCATE
(in **kul** kate)

> *Verb.* **To teach by repetition. To instill by persistent and constant instruction. To reiterate. To impress on someone's mind through forceful and repetitive instruction. To drill in. To implant in the mind.**
>
> • *She never wavered from her objective of **inculcating** the importance of traditional family values upon her children.*
>
> • *In breaking away from the control of the King of England, our American forefathers sought to **inculcate** a new mode of thinking and a new manner of action based on a government of, by and for the people.*

INDIGENOUS
(en **dij** uh nus)

> *Adj.* **Originating in a certain region of the country. Innate. Characteristic of a particular area.**
>
> • *The book describes trees and plants **indigenous** to the Southwest.*
>
> • *Our host prepared a meal with food **indigenous** to his native country.*

INDOLENT
(**en** duh lent)

> *Adj.* **Appearing to dislike activity or exertion. Lazy. Lethargic. Languid or unenergetic.**

• An **indolent** employee.

• The summer passed slowly with days that seemed to never end. He found himself in that **indolent**, but agreeable condition of doing absolutely nothing.

✪ The opposite of "indolent" is "productive," "busy," or "conscientious."

INEFFABLE
(en **eff** uh bul)

Adj. **That which cannot be stated or expressed. So astonishing, it cannot be put into words. Indescribable. Beyond description.**

• With the birth of her first child, she felt **ineffable** joy.

• It was a senseless accident that should never have happened, and all he could do was stare at the carnage in **ineffable** disgust.

INELUCTABLE
(**en** e **luk** tuh bul)

Adj. **Unavoidable. Inescapable. Inevitable. That which cannot be resisted. That which could be predicted or foretold.**

• The seemingly fearless nature of U. S. Navy pilots is most likely engendered by their feelings of **ineluctable** superiority in their training, their aircraft, and their supporting systems.

• Without knowledge of the impending storm, and

*without adequate navigation equipment, he set sail on the high seas; his tragic fate was **ineluctable**.*

INEXPLICABLY
(**en** x **plik** cuh blee)

> *Adv.* **Without explanation. Bizarrely. Enigmatically. Inscrutably. Strangely.**
>
> • *Even after all the positive recommendations were submitted, he **inexplicably** failed to approve the request.*
>
> • ***Inexplicably**, they did not show up for the final examination.*

INEXTRICABLE
(en **x** truh cuh bul)

> *Adj.* **That from which you cannot remove yourself. Unable to get disentangled or freed.**
>
> • *She found herself in an **inextricable** mess.*
>
> • *His message to the managers was clear and concise: stay focused on the ultimate goal, delegate as much as possible, and don't let yourself be trapped in that **inextricable** web of administrative details.*
>
> • *The name of Neil Armstrong, the first man to walk on the moon, has been **inextricably** (**adverbial form**) linked to the United States' space program.*

INFAMY
(**en** fuh me)

>*Noun.* **Negative notoriety. Scandal. Villainy or dishonor. Disgrace.**

>• *President Franklin Delano Roosevelt described December 7, 1941, as, "A day that will live in* **infamy***."*

>• *In Wichita, Kansas, Dennis Rader, identified as being the* **infamous** *(***adjectival form***) BTK serial killer, was sentenced to 10 consecutive life terms.*

INFLAMMABLE
(en **flam** uh bul)

>*Adj.* **Means the same thing as flammable. Easily set on fire. Combustible. More commonly, the word "inflammatory" is used to describe that which invokes strong human emotions, passion, anger, rage, or resentment.**

>• *As a precautionary measure, the* **inflammable** *materials were removed from the warehouse*

>• *His* **inflammatory** *remarks brought jeers from the audience.*

INGENIOUS
(en **jeen** yus)

>*Adj.* **Clever. Endowed with great skill. Inventive. That which shows inspiration and imagination. Resourceful.**

• *Using the customer's actual data during the presentation was an* **ingenious** *method of demonstrating the effectiveness of our products.*

• *Called the "Wizard of Menlo Park," Thomas Edison held over a thousand patents that included the incandescent light bulb, the phonograph and motion picture equipment. He is probably the most prolific and* **ingenious** *inventor in American history.*

INGENUOUS
(en **jen** u us)

> *Adj.* **Free from guile. Honest. Candid and sincere. Innocent. Straightforward. Openly frank. Lacking subtlety.**

• *A hand-written note, a bottle of sparkling champagne, and a single yellow rose; all were* **ingenuous** *declarations of his fondness for her.*

• *"Why can't I see God?" the young boy* **ingenuously** **(adverbial form)** *asked his father.*

When using this word, think of the naïve, innocent, and unrestrained qualities of a young child.

INIMITABLE
(en **em** uh tuh bul)

>*Adj.* **That which cannot be imitated or copied. Matchless. Peerless or incomparable. Truly unique.**
>
>• *Employing his own **inimitable** style, he executed the plan flawlessly.*
>
>• *Backed by an 88-piece symphony orchestra, he gave an **inimitable** performance that was much heralded by the critics.*

INNOCUOUS
(en **nok** u us)

>*Adj.* **Bland or inoffensive. That which is not harmful or injurious. Not detrimental to the whole. Harmless. Not likely to offend.**
>
>• *The attorney made only a few **innocuous** changes to the lease.*
>
>• *Even though most of the shareholders wanted specific information, the chairman confined himself to mostly **innocuous** generalities.*

INSIDIOUS
(en **sid** e us)

>*Adj.* **Stealthily treacherous. Subtle in manner, but perilous in effect. Sinister. Menacing.**
>
>• *It is an **insidious** physical disorder because it has so few symptoms.*

• *Don't coddle malcontents in your group. Their nega-tivism will spread like an* **insidious** *disease.*

INTREPID
(en **trep** id)

Adj. **Bold. Courageous. Valiant. Fearless. Dauntless, or brave.**

• *One has to marvel at the* **intrepid** *spirit of those early pioneers who forged westward with an unrelenting drive to survive in an ascetic world of hardship, violent weather, and limited provisions.*

• *Audie Murphy rose to national prominence as the most decorated combat soldier of World War II. He received 5 decorations from France and Belgium, and 33 awards and decorations from the United States. Among those awards was the Medal of Honor, the highest military award given by the United States for "conspicuous gal-lantry and* **intrepidity** **(noun form)** *at the risk of his life, above and beyond the call of duty."*

INVECTIVE
(en **vek** tiv)

Noun. **A diatribe. A strong criticism. A bitter denunciation. That which berates. A tirade.**

• *After being highly disappointed in the students' essays, the professor delivered a series of* **invectives** *berating their performances.*

✪   Two words that are the opposite of "invec-tive" are "praise" and "plaudit."

JABBERWOCKY

Nonsensical writing or speech usually done for comic relief. It is also the title of a poem in Lewis Carroll's *Through the Looking Glass.*

JADED
(**jay** did)

Adj. Tired or worn out by overwork or overuse. Surfeited or sated. Bored and cynical. Dulled by excess. No longer interesting because of overexposure.

• *Having been the manager of his group for so long, he became* **jaded** *in his approach to solving personnel issues.*

• *The old man is never pleasant to be around. His constant chatter will leave you* **jaded**.

JET STREAM

Very strong winds that encircle the globe several miles above the surface and generally move in a westerly to easterly direction. They can reach speeds up to 300 miles per hour. That is why it takes longer to fly in a westerly direction than to fly the same distance in an easterly direction.

JINGOISM

The policy, practice, or advocacy of boasting about a country's preparedness for war. Loud, blustering patriotism. The word is derived from the nickname "jingo" that was used to identify those who supported British naval action against the Russians in 1878.

JOLLY ROGER

A name given to a pirate's flag that displays the skull and crossbones.

JOLSON, AL

Born Asa Yoelson (1886–1950). Russian born American singer and film actor. He starred in the first full-length talking film, "The Jazz Singer" (1927). This movie signaled the end of the silent film era.

JUDICIOUS

(jew **dish** us)

Adj. Sound in judgment. Sensible. Prudent. Discreet.

• *A judicious use of one's time.*

• *A judicious approach to resolving a dispute.*

• *A judicious decision.*

JUNK BONDS

When a company wishes to raise money, e.g., to finance a takeover, they can issue bonds that carry a high interest rate but are judged to be a risky investment. The name is used to imply doubt about the company's ability to pay the interest from income generated by the acquired asset.

JUPITER

In Roman mythology, the highest or chief deity. In astronomy, it is the largest planet in our solar system with a diameter 11 times greater than the earth, but only 1/10th the size of the sun.

KILOMETER

In the metric system, it is a unit of measurement equaling 1000 meters. It is roughly equivalent to 3280 feet or about 5/8th of a mile (5280 feet). Thus, one meter is approximately 3.28 feet and as such is slightly longer than one yard. At first blush this appears difficult to retain. Just remember that a mile is longer than a kilometer, and a yard is shorter than a meter.

KING, MARTIN LUTHER

An American minister and civil rights leader. He advocated non-violent, peaceful protests against racial discrimination. He organized a march on Washington of 200,000 demonstrators in 1963, where he delivered his celebrated speech that began with, "I have a dream. . . ." He was awarded the Nobel Peace Prize in 1964 and was assassinated in 1968.

LABYRINTH
(**lab** uh rinth)

Noun. A maze. Any complicated or intricate network of paths or passages. A confusing or tortuous arrangement. A complex entanglement. A web.

• *Behind the large estate was a cobblestone path that wound through a **labyrinth** of native trees, flowers and ornamental shrubs.*

• *As a news correspondent reporting on a foreign government, he found himself immersed in a **labyrinth** of deceit, lies, espionage and intrigue.*

LACONIC
(luh **kon** ik)

> *Adj.* **Terse. Concise and to the point. Expressing much in few words. Pithy. Brief.**

> • *It would be an intriguing analysis to read if someone were to contrast the **laconic** style of Ernest Hemingway with the toilsome styles of many of today's modern writers.*

> •*Each group had its own special interests at stake, but the mediator arrived at a workable resolution with **laconic** precision.*

LAISSEZ FAIRE
(**lez** a **fare**)

> *Noun/Adj.* **(French) Literally, "allow to do." An economic theory that advocates little intervention or interference from the government on the workings of the market—clearly the hallmark of free market theories. The theory is based on the belief that the natural economic order, when not over-regulated or disturbed by artificial incentives, will result in the best possible conditions for the people.**

> • *The Republican Party has traditionally supported a position of **laissez-faire** capitalism, lower taxes and conservative social policies.*

By extension, the word also carries an attitudinal definition that describes an unwillingness to get involved. Not wanting to influence the actions of others. Refusing to interfere in the affairs of others. Preferring to remain on the sidelines.

• *There are many women's groups who believe an attitude of **laissez-faire** prevails in this country since there are so few laws on the books governing spousal abuse.*

LANGUISH
(**lang** guish)

Verb. **To be or to grow feeble. Lose vitality. To pine away. Droop. Lacking in activity. To become dispirited. To exist in a state of inactivity.**

• *The stock **languished** under the pressures of a down market.*

• *After **languishing** in obscurity for a number of years, his literary efforts finally started to gain national attention.*

✪   The opposite of "languish" is "flourish."

LATENT
(**lay** tent)

Adj. **Present but not obvious. Hidden. Concealed. Not readily apparent. Suppressed. Not observable or evident.**

• *The building had certain **latent** defects that were not uncovered during the initial inspection.*

• *He was diagnosed as having **latent** homicidal tendencies.*

LATITUDE
(**lat** uh **tude**)

Noun. **The distance on a meridian north or south of the equator measured in degrees and minutes. More commonly, it refers to freedom from restrictions. Wide parameters for performing some action.**

• *He was given ample **latitude** to effect a change.*

• *The design specifications were so unconstrained that it allowed the designers a great deal of **latitude** to express their creativity.*

LATTER-DAY SAINTS

Mormons are members of the Church of Jesus Christ of Latter-day Saints. This is a religious movement founded in New York State in 1830 by Joseph Smith. Brigham Young, who moved the Mormon headquarters to Salt Lake City, Utah, in 1847, followed him into office. The official name of the church is based on their belief that Jesus Christ is the Son of God and central to their worship. The term "Latter-day Saints" is a reference to a latter period of time and is a countertype expression to the saints of the older Christian Church, i.e., former-day saints. They are called Mormons because of their belief in the Book of Mormons as the Word of God.

LAUDABLE
(**lau** duh bul)

Adj. That which is praiseworthy. Commendable. Exemplary.

• *She was from a small town in Oklahoma, but her performance on American Idol captured the hearts of the nation with a **laudable** performance that will be remembered for years.*

• *Even though they fell short of their goal, it was a **laudable** effort.*

LAY/LIE
These two verbs have been included in this endeavor since people continue to be confused over the proper use of each.

First, let's define the basic differences between each verb. "Lay" is a transitive verb. That means it requires a direct object. The subject of the sentence must act on something. For example: "The hen lays an egg." In this case, the hen is the subject and the egg is the direct object.

"Lie" is an intransitive verb. It does not require a direct object. The subject of the sentence does not act on something. For example: "She wants to lie down." In this case, she is the subject of the sentence and there is no direct object.

Secondly, we must know the principal parts of each verb. For purposes of this entry, we will focus only on the Present and Past Tenses.

Present Tense	Past Tense	Present Participle	Past Participle
Lay	Laid	Laying	Laid
Lie	Lay	Lying	Lain

Most of the confusion surrounding these two words comes from the fact that the past tense of "lie" is "lay," the same as the present tense of "lay." Thus:

• *You may **lay** your briefcase on the table*–**Present Tense.**

• *Yesterday, you **laid** your briefcase on the table*–**Past Tense.**

• *I **lie** in the sun every day*–**Present Tense.**

• *Yesterday, I **lay** in the sun all day*–**Past Tense.**

The last example listed is the one most often mis-used. You are being grammatically incorrect if you say, "Yesterday, I laid in the sun all day" since the past tense of "lie" is "lay." The correct usage would be, "Yesterday, I lay in the sun all day."

AUTHOR'S NOTE

Armed with this information, recognize that the next time you tell your dog to "Lay down!"— and it refuses to obey—it may be just waiting for you to use the proper verb.

LEEWARD

Chiefly nautical term meaning on or toward the side sheltered from the wind, i.e., the lee side. The opposite side (the side the wind is coming from) is referred to as the windward side.

LEGREE, SIMON

The mean and brutal slave dealer in Harriet Beecher Stowe's classic novel *Uncle Tom's Cabin*. The book is a fictionalized portrayal of the misery and sadness of blacks in nineteenth century America, and at the time served as a significant propaganda tool for anti-slavery factions. Metaphorically, a Simon Legree refers to any person who is a stern or harsh taskmaster.

LEITMOTIF

(**lite** mo **teef**)

In both musical and literary compositions, it is a recurring theme associated with a particular person, situation or idea. The poignant and haunting music that is played every time the phantom appears in the musical "Phantom Of The Opera", and the unsettling theme of the shark's appearances in the movie "Jaws" are good examples of leitmotif.

LETHARGIC

(luh **thar** jik)

Adj. Sluggish. Languid. A feeling of weariness or listlessness. A lack of vitality or energy. Phlegmatic. Apathetic and indifferent.

• *The convention was in full swing, but he felt too* **lethargic** *to attend any of the sessions.*

• *The* **lethargic** *alligator was no threat to the ducks.*

LEWIS, SINCLAIR

American novelist (1885–1951). Gained fame for his social satires on small town life in the Midwest. Popular novels include *Main Street, Babbit,* and *Elmer Gantry.* He was the first American writer to be awarded the Nobel Prize for literature.

LIBRETTO

(luh **bret** o)

The text or words of any extended, musical and vocal composition. A librettist is the author of the words. In a musical, the word "book" is used to refer to the words. Oscar Hammerstein of the celebrated Rogers and Hammerstein musical team would be considered a librettist.

LICENTIOUS

(lie **sin** shus)

Adj. Disregardful of any sense of law or morality. Lewd. Going beyond proper behavior. Immoral. Having no regard for accepted standards. Decadent or depraved. Lascivious.

• *Unfortunately, he was known more for his* **licentious** *behavior than for his noteworthy accomplishments.*

• *It is the hilarious story of three down-and-out, coarse, and* **licentious** *men who are taken in by a group of nuns until they can get back on their feet.*

LIMERICK
(**lem** er ik)

A comical or humorous verse of five lines. Reportedly named after a refrain in a song "Will you come up to Limerick," meaning Limerick, Ireland. Limericks are structured where the first, second and fifth lines rhyme with each other, and the third and fourth are shorter and rhyme with each other.

• *There once was a fellow named Lancelot*
Who liked to play golf with his friends a lot
But try as he might
His ball always went right
So his buddies called him Sir Shanks-a-lot.

LIMPID
(**lem** pid)

Adj. When referring to someone's eyes or to water or something similar, it means clear or transparent. Not obscured. Crystal clear. Free from flaws or blemishes.

• *For her birthday, he presented her with a sterling silver bracelet mounted with brilliant emeralds and **limpid** diamonds.*

When used to describe something that is written, it means clear, easy to understand. Lucid. Comprehendible.

• *Even though the subject matter was complex, the professor commended him for his clear, **limpid** style of writing.*

LINGUISTICS
(ling **gwis** tiks)

Noun. **The scientific study of language. It encompasses phonetics, syntax, form and structure. It analyzes historical changes and trends and the influences of other languages.**

• *She told all who would listen that her major field of study at the university would be* **linguistics.**

• *The* **linguistics** *professor made an extensive excursion into Alaska to study the language of the Inuit.*

LITERALLY
(**lit** er uh lee)

Adv. **Means "word for word." In the exact sense of the word. Without exaggeration or metaphor. Exactly.**

• *The village was* **literally** *destroyed.*

• *Most Christian groups who consider themselves fundamentalist believe in a* **literal** (**adjectival form**) *interpretation of the Bible.*

The adverb "figuratively" (fig yur a tive lee**) has almost the opposite meaning of "literally." It is not in the exact sense as is "literally." It means symbolically, metaphorically or emblematically.**

• *Figuratively, his refusal to cooperate is a shot across the bow.*

In the example above, his refusal to cooperate

serves as a warning that something is amiss and is referred to figuratively in this example as a "shot across the bow."

LITERATI
(**lit** uh **rah** tee)
> *Noun.* A collective expression meaning scholarly or learned people. The intelligentsia. Clerisy. The well educated.

> • *While most of his works had received little national acclaim, he was well known among the **literati**.*

> ### AUTHOR'S NOTE
> It should be noted that this word is sometimes used in an uncomplimentary manner to disparage or belittle members of this group.

> • *Only those who consider themselves among the **literati** would want to read such a tedious book.*

LITIGIOUS
(luh **tij** us)
> *Adj.* Pertaining to litigation. Secondarily, it means overly inclined to file a lawsuit. Eager to contest in a court of law.

> • *Unfortunately, we live in a **litigious** society where the least inconvenience is cause for a lawsuit.*

> • *Because of the prevailing notion that **litigious** actions are an easy way to make money, it is no longer a ques–*

*tion of being right or wrong. **Today, you're either right or you're sued.***

LOQUACIOUS
(low **kway** shus)

Adj. Talkative. Voluble. Garrulous. Inclined to talk often and freely.

• *He is very **loquacious** and will at times annoy those around him.*

The opposite of "loquacious" is "reticent" (**ret** uh sent), **an adjective that describes a person who is reluctant to speak or quiet and uncommunicative.**

LORAN

A system of long-range navigation where your position is determined by the interval of time that has elapsed between two known radio transmissions. The name is derived from *lo*ng *ra*nge *n*avigation.

LOX
(**locks**)

Noun. Smoked salmon. Typically eaten with cream cheese and bagels. (Yiddish *laks*)

LUGUBRIOUS
(lu **gu** bree us)

Adj. Mournful. Dismal. Expressive of sorrow. Depressing and sad, especially to an exaggerated degree.

• *He knew instantly that something was amiss when he heard the **lugubrious** sound of her voice.*

• *It has been reported in the news media that in some small foreign countries when the leader of the country passes away, mourners are paid to line the streets and express themselves in a **lugubrious** manner.*

Remember this word by thinking how sad and discouraging it is to have to change a flat tire. One of the first steps is to loosen the (*lug*) nuts.

LUMINARY
(**loo** muh nary)

Noun. A natural light-giving source like the sun or the moon. More commonly, it is used to describe any individual that is intellectually enlightening or a provider of inspiration. It also means a prominent or famous person. A person who inspires others. Someone who enlightens mankind, e.g., Albert Einstein. A celebrity.

• *Each year, the Academy Awards ceremony offers the movie buff an opportunity to see a large number of Hollywood **luminaries**.*

LUSITANIA

A British steamship that was sunk by a German submarine in the north Atlantic in May 1915. Over 1000 lives were lost. This precipitated strong anti-German feelings in the United States and was one of the events that prompted the United States to enter the First World War.

LYCEUM
(lie **see** em)
>A garden with covered walkways in Athens where Aristotle taught philosophy. In the United States it refers to any literary institution, lecture hall or the like where instruction is given by lectures and other means.

MACH NUMBER
>A number that describes the ratio between an object's air speed (usually an airplane) and the speed of sound. A plane flying at mach two would be flying at twice the speed of sound. At sea level, the speed of sound is approximately 750 miles per hour.

MADAME BUTTERFLY
>An opera composed by Giacomo Puccini (1858–1924). The score is rich and dramatic, but the opera itself is very different than most operas. The plot is simple and straight line, without the fanfare and spectacle you might expect. Japanese girl meets United States Navy officer, loses him, then commits suicide. The musical, *Miss Saigon*, is loosely based on this opera by Puccini.

MAE WEST
>An inflatable life jacket for those who have fallen into the sea. So named as an allusion to the large bust of actress Mae West.

MAGNANIMOUS
(mag **nan** uh mus)

Adj. **High minded. Noble. Not petty or vindictive in conduct. Forgiving of insults and injuries.**

• *Despite the verbal assaults, he was **magnanimous** in his responses.*

• *The CEO chose to **magnanimously** (**adverbial form**) overlook the insolent behavior of the systems engineering manager.*

MAINSTREAM
(**main stream**)

Noun. **The prevailing course or trend in fashion, music, opinions, etc.**

• *Today, rap artists together with female divas such as Britney Spears and Mariah Carey represent the **mainstream** of American pop culture.*

MAL-

A prefix meaning "bad" or "ill." It attributes its meaning to the second element of the word as in maladjusted—meaning to be poorly adjusted to something.

MALADROIT
(**mal** uh **droit**)

Adj. **Clumsy. Awkward. Someone who is all thumbs or is unskillful. Inept.**

• *We have practiced every day for the last two weeks,*

*but he is still unusually **maladroit** at completing the exercise.*

• *His **maladroit** execution of the shot surprised everyone, including the television commentators.*

MALCONTENT
(**mal** kun **tent**)

Noun/Adj. **Someone who is always unhappy with things as they are. Always dissatisfied. A complainer. A whiner.**

• *The Major's first assessment of his troops was that, unequivocally, they were a deplorable group of indolent **malcontents**.*

The adjective "malcontented" (mal kun **tent** ed) **is used to describe this type of person. One who is malcontented and unusually negative.**

• *He is a **malcontented** individual who always sees the half empty glass.*

MALIGN
(muh **line**)

Verb/Adj. **As a verb it means to speak ill of someone. To slander someone. To smear their name or character.**

• *The magazine article **maligned** both his vision for the company and his ability to manage it.*

As an adjective it means hurtful or pernicious in effect.

• *The much-maligned politician responded vociferously to the accusations.*

MANDARIN
(**man** duh ren)
>There are a number of dialects spoken in China. Mandarin is the most widely spoken group of dialects and is the official language of China.

MANDATORY
(**man** duh **tor** e)
>*Adj.* That which must be done. Obligatory. Compulsory. Required.

>• *It is **mandatory** that the assignments be completed on time.*

>• *It was only a matter of time before baseball would require **mandatory** drug testing of its players.*

>• *The Board of Directors approved a resolution lowering the **mandatory** retirement age to 62 years of age.*

MANIFEST
(**man** uh **fest**)
>*Verb/Adj./Noun.* Clear or obvious. Readily perceptible by the mind. Clear to the eye. Plainly evident. Easily noticed.

>• *His ability to act calmly under pressure **manifested***

(verb form) *itself in the manner in which he handled the emergency.*

• *There was* **manifest** **(adjectival form)** *disgust among the workers when the plant manager abolished the free lunch program.*

As a noun it is a list of such things as cargo on a ship or passengers on an airplane.

• *The* **manifest** *indicated that an additional 5 tons of steel parts had been added to the cargo hold.*

The word "manifestation" is a noun meaning the act of that which is existing or happening. That which is indicated, manifested, or demonstrated.

• *The rise in the unemployment rate was further* **manifestation** *of a weakening economy.*

AUTHOR'S NOTE

Our American history books contain the term Manifest Destiny. This was a doctrine believed by those at the time that the United States had both an immutable right and an obligation to expand across the North American continent.

MARCH HARE

March is the breeding season for hares. During this time, excessive jumping, immoderate movements and overall strange behavior characterize their actions. Hence, the expression, "Wild as a March hare."

MARGINALIZE
(**mar** juh nuh lize)
> *Verb.* To make or treat something as insignificant. To trivialize. To refer to something as not important or of no consequence. To diminish the significance. To relegate to a marginal or less important position.
>
> • *We were upset over his attempts to* **marginalize** *our efforts.*
>
> • *The foreign troops have occupied the small country for so long that its native language has been* **marginalized***.*
>
> • *The White House issued a press release in an attempt to* **marginalize** *the criticism it had received over the Vice President's statements.*

MARSHALL PLAN
> A plan initiated by George Marshall who served as a general in the army during World War II and as Secretary of State after the war. The plan called for financial and other aid to Western European countries whose economies had been harmed and weakened by the war. Marshall was awarded the Nobel Peace Prize in 1953.

MARTINET
(**mar** tuh **net**)
> *Noun.* A description or expression given to someone who is a strict disciplinarian. Someone rigid and controlling. One who insists that rules and

orders always be obeyed even in those instances where it is neither necessary nor practical

• *With his authoritative and over-bearing mannerisms, he appears more a **martinet** than a university professor.*

> ### AUTHOR'S NOTE
> The word is derived from General Martinet, who was a strict drillmaster in the French army.

MASON-DIXON LINE

The boundary line between Maryland and Pennsylvania originally mapped by surveyors Charles Mason and Jeremiah Dixon, and later applied to the entire southern boundary of Pennsylvania. Before the abolishment of slavery, it was considered the dividing line between free and slave states.

MATRICULATE

(muh **trik** u late)

Verb. **To admit or enroll in a college or university.**

• *Each year, thousands of students are **matriculated** into various colleges and universities across the nation.*

MAVERICK

The name is ascribed to an animal that is found without a brand. More commonly, it refers to an individual whose actions are unorthodox or outside of normal behavior. An independent-minded person. The name comes from Samuel Maverick, a Texas cattle rancher who refused to brand his cattle.

McCARTHYISM
An aggressive campaign from 1950 - 1954 to uncover communists within the U. S. government and other institutions. It was led by Senator Joseph McCarthy. Many referred to this campaign as a "witch hunt." Most of those accused were totally innocent, but many lost their jobs and were blacklisted. The hysteria this created finally ceased after McCarthy was publicly censured in 1954.

MEIN KAMPF
(mine **kampf**)
(German) *My Struggle:* The autobiography of Adolf Hitler, the Austrian born Nazi leader and Chancellor of Germany from 1933 to 1945. It outlines his political beliefs and sets forth his plan for the conquest of Europe.

MELVILLE, HERMAN
(1819–1891) American novelist, essayist, and short story writer. Best known for having written *Moby Dick* (1851), which he dedicated to his friend and fellow writer, Nathaniel Hawthorne.

MENDACIOUS
(men **day** shus)
Adj. Untruthful. False. Given to misrepresent-

ing the truth. Deceitful. Characterized by lies. Misleading.

• *The attorney was convinced that the witness had just given a* **mendacious** *account of his involvement in the events.*

• *She was forced to defend herself from* **mendacious** *accusations made by those who were jealous of her success.*

✪   The opposite of "mendacious" is "truthful" or "honest."

METAPHOR
(met uh **for**)

Noun. A figure of speech that applies a name or description to an object, person, or action that is not literally applicable. Metaphors are used for colorful and dramatic effect.

• *It was a stone-cold lie.*

In this example, we know that a lie does not have a temperature. But with the use of the descriptor, "stone-cold," we know it was something more than a little white lie.

When two or more incompatible metaphors are employed, it is called a mixed metaphor. It occurs when the parts of the comparison don't match.

• *The governor turned the ship of state on its heels.*

In this example, "ship" and "heels" do not compare.

• *Resolutions to their problems seem clouded in a sea of distrust.*

In this example, "clouded" and "sea" do not compare. By substituting the word "fog" for "sea," a favorable comparison is made.

• *Resolutions to their problems seem clouded in a fog of disturst.*

While the use of metaphors is a colorful way of expressing the action, be careful when using them. They can become awkward and sometimes not easily understood.

Also, do not confuse a metaphor with a simile. A simile is a figure of speech that expresses a resemblance of one thing to another.

• *"She had lips like cherry wine."*

• *"He is as strong as a bull."*

A simile always uses the words "like" or "as" in its construction.

METICULOUS
(muh **tik** u lis)

Adj. Excessively attentive to details. Precise. Finically careful.

• She is **meticulous** about her appearance.

• His **meticulous** examination of the case left no room for error.

MIDWAY ISLANDS

A group of small islands in the Pacific Ocean near the northwestern end of the Hawaiian archipelago. They are located about one third of the distance between Honolulu and Tokyo. It was here in June of 1942 that the United States defeated the Japanese in a decisive naval engagement. Many consider this victory the turning point in the war with Japan.

MINDLESSLY

(**mind** lis lee)

Adv. Carelessly. Heedlessly. Without forethought or study. Imprudently. Without using intelligence. Senselessly.

• He **mindlessly** overlooked an essential component of the solution.

• A few of the students were **mindlessly** throwing water balloons at passing cars.

• It was a violent film full of **mindless** (**adjectival form**) brutality.

✪   The opposite of "mindlessly" is "deliberately."

MIS-

A prefix meaning "ill" or "wrong." It is also applied to anything bad or anything having a negative force.

MISCONSTRUE
(miss kun **strue**)

Verb. **To interpret wrongly. To misread. To misunderstand. To get the wrong impression.**

• *From his actions, he obviously* **misconstrued** *the purpose of the directive.*

• *The report must be carefully worded so that there is no chance it will be* **misconstrued**.

MISANTHROPE
(**miss** en **thrope**)

Noun. **A person who hates people. One who attempts to avoid society as a whole. A person who distrusts others.**

MISOGAMIST
(muh **sog** uh mist)

Noun. **One who hates marriage.**

MISOGYNIST
(muh **sog** uh nist)

Noun. **One who hates women.**

MITIGATE
(**mit** uh **gate**)

Verb. **To make less intense or less severe. To alleviate. To ease the severity. To lessen or take the edge off.**

• *The purpose of the legislation is to* **mitigate** *the tax burden on lower income families.*

• *After Hurricane Katrina made landfall, the food and supplies flown in by the Red Cross helped* **mitigate** *the suffering of those who lived along the Gulf Coast.*

• *He has been an effective employee for a number of years, so you have to wonder if there were any* **mitigating** (adjectival form) *circumstances surrounding his unseemly behavior.*

MODERN ENGLISH
The English language from about 1500 onward.

MOMENTARY
(**moe** men **tare** e)

Adj. **Lasting only a brief period of time. Short-lived. Fleeting.**

• *The first chapter of the book provided only a* **momentary** *glimpse of his boyhood life.*

• *A* **momentary** *hesitation.*

• *We will begin the presentation* **momentarily** (adverbial form).

MONROE DOCTRINE

A principle of foreign policy of the United States during the presidency of President James Monroe. It offered that any intervention or hostile act by a European colonial power against any country in the Americas would potentially be viewed as a hostile act against the United States.

MONUMENTAL
(**mon** u **men** tul)

Adj. More commonly used to denote massive, large or very imposing. It is also used to refer to something significant or prominent.

• *We were in awe of the **monumental** sculptures that stood in the gardens surrounding the estate.*

• *The creation of the jet engine was a **monumental** event in the history of aviation.*

MORDANT
(**more** dent)

Adj. Caustic. Sarcastic. Biting. Sardonic and cynical.

• *He had a **mordant** sense of humor.*

• *His **mordant** comments were further proof that he lacked the necessary aplomb to be an effective manager.*

MORIBUND
(**more** uh **bund**)

Adj. **Near death. In a dying condition. Lacking vitality. On its last legs.**

• *The ambulance delivered him to the emergency room in an unconscious and **moribund** state.*

• *With new developments occurring almost daily, the old, established principles are now **moribund**.*

MUNDANE
(mun **dane**)

Adj. **Pertaining to the world or the earth. More commonly used to denote something dull and routine. Customary. Ordinary or commonplace.**

• *His daily life lacked excitement. He spent most of his time performing **mundane** activities.*

• *As a sales person, he had felt the excitement and thrill of closing large transactions. Since being promoted to sales manager, he found little elation in completing the **mundane** administrative requirements of the job.*

MUSE
(**muze**)

Noun/Verb. **The primary meaning of the word is as a noun. In Greek mythology, Muse is one of the nine daughters of Zeus and Mnemosyne. The daughters inspire those who pursue creative endeavors. Therefore, a guiding spirit. One who provides ideas and inspiration.**

• *She not only modeled for his paintings, but was also his* **muse**.

As a verb it means to ponder or reflect. To meditate in silence. To cogitate. To mull over.

• *Sometimes in the quiet solitude of the night, he* **mused** *over the countless mistakes he had made in his life and wished somehow he could turn back the hands of time.*

MYRIAD
(**mear** e id)
> *Noun.* **Countless. Numerous. A great number of people or things. An infinite amount.**

> • *He had a* **myriad** *of excuses in an attempt to explain his absence.*

> • *This branch office has been beset with a* **myriad** *of problems ranging from inadequate facilities to high attrition.*

✪   The opposite of "myriad" is "few."

MYTHICAL
(**mith** uh cul)
> *Adj.* **Pertaining to myths. More commonly, the word is used to describe something fictitious or having no foundation in fact. Imaginary. Something not supported by actual conditions.**

> • *In medieval art, the* **mythical** *unicorn was depicted as an animal that resembled a white horse with a single horn protruding from its forehead.*

• *His purported influence with members of the board of regents is completely* **mythical**.

NARRATIVE
(**nare** uh tive)
> A spoken or written account that tells a story, whether true or fictitious, of events or experiences typically in the order of happening. It can be present, past or future; short or long.

N.A.T.O.
> North Atlantic Treaty Organization. It is an association of European and North American countries for the mutual protection of its members from any aggression posed by another country.

NATURAL SELECTION
> An evolutionary process proposed by Charles Darwin in his 1859 publication, *On the Origin of Species*. It suggests that some varieties of a particular species within a total population might be better adapted to their surroundings and would therefore continue to live and prosper. This is the pure meaning of "survival of the fittest."

NAUTICAL MILE
> A unit of distance measurement used in maritime navigation equaling 2,025 yards as compared to a statute mile that equals 1,760 yards (5280 feet). The term for the rate of speed over a nautical mile is referred to as a knot. To convert knots to miles per hour use the following conversion factor (1 knot = 1.15077945 miles per hour). Thus, a

, Navy jet fighter landing on an aircraft car-
with a landing speed of 130 knots would be
eling approximately 150 miles per hour.

NEBULOUS
(**neb** u lus)

> *Adj.* Vague. Without form. Indistinct. Hazy. Ill-
> defined or imprecise. Unclear. Uncertain. Lacking
> definition. Obscure.

AUTHOR'S NOTE
This is an actual entry from a naval diary.

• *"When the ship was in port, Ensign Weir would oftentimes leave the ship on his own volition and without
permission. No one knew he was leaving or where he
was going. It became so commonplace that if you could
not locate a shipmate on board, it was sometimes said,
'He must be taking a Weir.' A 'Weir' was that* **nebulous**
*area somewhere between being on vacation and being
A.W.O.L."* (**Absent Without Leave**).

• *The details he provided were sketchy at best, so he
obviously has a* **nebulous** *recollection of what transpired at the meeting.*

NEFARIOUS
(nuh **fare** e us)

> *Adj.* Extremely wicked. Immoral. Fiendish. Vile.
> Detestable or despicable. Shameful.

• *These are* **nefarious** *acts, and their perpetrators will
be brought to justice.*

• *He was found guilty of various **nefarious** schemes that defrauded the government of millions of dollars.*

NEO-

A word element meaning "new" or "modern." When you read or hear a reference to such things as Neo-Darwinism or Neo-Impressionism, it simply means newer and more modern ideas and techniques have been added to the movement while still maintaining the integrity of the original concept.

NEW ENGLAND

It is *not* just a general area in the northeast portion of the United States. It is a defined area comprising six states: Vermont, Massachusetts, Connecticut, Rhode Island, New Hampshire and Maine. It was so named by the English explorer, John Smith, in 1614.

NIGHTINGALE, FLORENCE
(1820–1910)

An English nurse. She became known world wide for leading a movement to dramatically improve public health and hospital care.

NOBEL, ALFRED B.

A Swedish chemist and engineer. He invented dynamite and manufactured other new explosives. In the process he amassed a large fortune that he used to endow the prizes that bear his name. Annually, Nobel prizes are awarded for physics, chemistry, literature, and medicine, and to the individual adjudged to have rendered the greatest services to the cause of peace. The latter, a seemingly ironic endeavor for a man who invented explosives.

NOM DE PLUME
(**nom** duh **ploom**)
> (French) Literally, "name of pen." Pen name. An author's invented name. Author's pseudonym.

NOMINAL
(**nom** uh nul)
> *Adj.* Existing in name only. So-called. Not real. Ostensibly.

> • *Considering that violent outbursts were still occurring throughout many parts of the country, the ceasefire represented a **nominal** cessation of the war.*

> • *He is the **nominal** head of the department, but the middle managers do most of the decision-making.*

> When used to describe costs or expenditures, it means small in relation to the value received. Virtually nothing.

> • *They charged a **nominal** fee.*

NON-CONFORMITY
(**non** kun **form** uh tee)
> *Noun.* Not doing the accepted thing. Not conventional or traditional. A failure to conform.

• *This sort of **non-conformity** is not consistent with our history or our tradition and accordingly will not be tolerated at this institution.*

• *She had been raised in a family that stressed traditional family values, and her occasional acts of **non-conformity** brought a quick response from her parents.*

NON-DESCRIPT
(**non** duh **skript**)

Adj. **A person or thing that lacks distinctive features or characteristics. Not recognized as a particular type or classification. Not similar in appearance to that which is typical.**

• *Even though his appearance was **non-descript**, he delivered an effective presentation.*

• *After further investigation, it was found that the software contained numerous **non-descript** flaws.*

NONETHELESS
(**nun** thu **less**)

Adv. **However. Despite that to the contrary. Nevertheless.**

• *While we have met our sales objectives for the year, **nonetheless,** we should continue to upgrade the quality and effectiveness of our presentations.*

• *Even though the city was still ravaged by the effects of the hurricane, **nonetheless**, he felt it was time to return home.*

NONPLUSED
(non **plused**)

>*Verb.* **Completely perplexed. Confused. Puzzled. Baffled or bewildered.**

>• *He was **nonplused** after reading the complex instructions.*

>• *She was in a state of **nonplus** (noun form) after learning of his decision to resign from the company.*

NOTEWORTHY
(**note wur** thee)

>*Adj.* **Notable. Important. Something worth mentioning. Attention-getting. Something of note.**

>• *His contributions to the goals of the group are **noteworthy**.*

>• *It is **noteworthy** that a sizeable number of our students are National Merit scholars.*

> ✪ The opposite of "noteworthy" is "insignificant."

NUGATORY
(**new** guh **tor** e)

>*Adj.* **It means of little importance or value. Worthless. Futile or trifling. Valueless. Useless in its effect. Inconsequential.**

>• *While he presented logical arguments in support of his position, his efforts to change their minds were **nugatory**.*

• *The new quarterly sales incentives obviously had a* **nugatory** *effect on sales results.*

OBJECTIONABLE
(ub **jek** shun uh bul)

Adj. **That which could be objected to or opposed. It is also used to describe something offensive. Unpleasant. Distasteful or unacceptable.**

• *We felt portions of the new movie were very* **objectionable***.*

• *Most of the* **objectionable** *and non-supportive comments he made concerning the new initiative have proven to be without merit.*

OBJET D'ART
(ob zhah **dar**)

(French) An object of art. A statue. A painting, etc.

OBLIGATORY
(uh **blig** uh **tor** e)

Adj. **Mandatory. Compulsory. That which is morally or legally binding. Required.**

• *After making the* **obligatory** *introduction of the members of his group, the speaker began his presentation.*

• *The company required all applicants to submit to an* **obligatory** *drug test prior to employment.*

OBSCURE
(ob **skure**)

> *Verb/Adj.* **As a verb it means to make less visible. To make unclear. To make something difficult to see.**

> • *Both the cloud cover and the reflective lights of the city **obscured** our view of the passing comet.*

As an adjective it means not plainly seen. Vague. Unclear. Not readily perceived. Inconspicuous or unnoticed.

> • *History will show it as the **obscure** beginnings of a new political movement.*

It can also mean of no distinction or prominence. Unknown.

> • *He was an **obscure** actor who burst onto the scene seemingly overnight.*

OBTUSE
(ob **toose**)

> *Adj.* **When used to describe a thing or an object, it means not sharp or acute. (An obtuse angle exceeds 90 degrees but is less than 180 degrees). When used to describe people, it means dull in perception, undiscerning, stupid or dim-witted.**

> • *Judging from his comments, he is too **obtuse** to comprehend the implications of his actions.*

The adjective "abstruse" (ab struse) presented earlier in this text is sometimes confused with "obtuse." Recall that "abstruse" means something difficult to understand. Recondite. Hard to comprehend.

• *The professor's lectures were oftentimes so **abstruse** that some students fell asleep in the middle of them.*

> **AUTHOR'S NOTE**
> Remember both words with the following statement. "It is too abstruse for someone so obtuse."

OBVIATE
(**ob** vee **ate**)

> *Verb.* To get around or dispose of a need. To avoid an inconvenience or problem by some particular action.

> • *By acquiring certain companies and their assets, we **obviated** the need to develop our own prototype.*

> • *Finding a peaceful resolution to the problems between the two countries would **obviate** the necessity of sending in United Nations military forces.*

OFF-CHANCE
(**off chance**)

> *Noun.* Remote possibility. Outside chance. Likelihood. Bare possibility.

• *Prepare summary reports for each of the members on the **off- chance** they will all be in attendance.*

• *There is an **off-chance** we will not be able to attend the awards banquet.*

OLD HICKORY

A nickname given to Andrew Jackson, a U.S. general and 7th President of the United States. He was not, however the only Jackson in American history that had a nickname. Thomas Jonathan Jackson was a confederate general during the civil war. He earned the nickname "Stonewall Jackson" at the first Battle of Bull Run where his troops stood like a stone wall.

OMEGA
(o **meg** uh)

Noun. The last letter of the Greek alphabet. Alpha is the first. Alpha and omega are sometimes used idiomatically as in the following:

• *It was the alpha and the **omega**—meaning it was the beginning and the end.*

OMINOUS
(**om** uh nus)

Adj. Threatening. Foreboding. Menacing. Inauspicious. That which is frightening and portentous. Presaging ill fortune.

• *He was concerned over the **ominous** rumble of discontent among the group.*

• *An **ominous** silence fell over the room as he announced that personnel cuts might be needed because of declining sales.*

✪   The opposite of "ominous" is "promising."

OMNI-
A word element meaning "all."

OMNIPRESENT
(**om** nee **prez** ent)
> *Adj.* It means existing everywhere at the same time. All-enveloping. All-pervading. All-embracing.

> • *An **omnipresent** deity.*

> • *The condition seems **omnipresent**.*

OMNIA VINCIT AMOR
(Latin) Love conquers all.

ONEROUS
(**on** er us)
> *Adj.* Burdensome. Oppressive. Imposing. That which is not easily handled. Taxing. Cumbersome.

> • *It is that time of the year when she is once again faced with the **onerous** task of preparing her income tax return.*

> • *He felt there were many provisions within the lease that were too **onerous** to be acceptable.*

✪   The opposite of "onerous" is "effortless," "easy," or "simple."

OPEC

This acronym stands for Organization of the Petroleum Exporting Countries. It is an international organization of eleven countries that rely heavily on revenues from exporting oil. The current members of OPEC include Algeria, Indonesia, Iran, Iraq, Kuwait, Libya, Nigeria, Qatar, Saudi Arabia, The United Arab Emirates and Venezuela. These eleven members supply about 40% of the world's oil output. They also possess approximately 75% of the total proven crude oil reserves. Since this is a vital world commodity, the Oil and Energy Ministers of OPEC meet twice a year to decide on output levels. Their goal is to bring stability to the oil market by ensuring a balance between supply and demand. They consider any adjustments that might be required depending on oil market developments. In the years ahead, it will become more and more difficult for OPEC to operate effectively if you believe in what some industry experts call "peak oil." This is that point in time when worldwide oil production will be declining because of diminished reserves. If this happens—and there are those in the industry who argue that this point will not occur until well into the future—it would create an international financial catastrophe. All modern economies would be dramatically affected. Mark Savinar reports in his enlightening article, "Life After the Oil Crash," that the Saudis have an expression that describes the glum outlook:

"My father rode a camel. I drive a car. My son flies a jet airplane. My grandson will ride a camel."

OPPORTUNE
(**op** er **tune**)

Adj. Appropriate. Timely. Suitable to the occasion. Occurring at a favorable time.

• *With the market growing, it seems an* **opportune** *time to expand our marketing services.*

• *This may be an* **opportune** *moment to discuss the financial considerations of the contract.*

OPPRESSIVE
(o **press** ive)

Adj. Burdensome. Taxing. Onerous. That which is difficult to endure. Arduous.

• *The* **oppressive** *heat of the summer months forced construction supervisors to have their crews on site at the break of dawn.*

• *At this company, the pressure to meet assigned quotas is* **oppressive**.

OSTENSIBLY
(os **ten** suh blee)

Adv. Apparently, but not necessarily true or real. Seemingly. Supposedly. That which is professed.

• **Ostensibly**, *he is in charge, but the real power within the organization rests with the Executive Committee.*

• *He was here* **ostensibly** *to offer his assistance, but it appears he was really here to get information on our plans.*

OUTLANDISH
(out **lan** dish)

Adj. **Bizarre. Highly peculiar. Wacky. That which is abnormally strange. The word can be used to describe places, practices, people, etc.**

• *Considering it was a very formal affair, the manner in which he dressed was* **outlandish**.

• *I can understand why she is upset. His was an* **outlandish** *response to her very legitimate question.*

OVERSHADOW
(o vur **shad** o)

Verb. **To cast into shade. More commonly, the word means to appear more prominent or to appear more important. To outshine. To outdo. To render insignificant by comparison.**

• *Her performance* **overshadowed** *those of all other contenders.*

• *While he shared in the family pride for his older brother, he always felt* **overshadowed** *by his accomplishments.*

OVERSIGHT
(**o** vur **site**)

Noun. **This word has two primary meanings. The**

first is an omission. A failure to notice. A failure to consider. A mistake. An inadvertent error.

• *It was an **oversight** that his name was not included on the invitation list.*

The second meaning of the word is supervision or management control.

• *The State Attorney General's office will provide general **oversight** to the investigation.*

P's & Q's

This is an English idiom that means something to be mindful of or to watch. To be attentive to. It is still in wide use today. There have been many explanations of how the phrase originated, but the most likely is that it started in Irish taverns and pubs that referred to the "pints" and "quarts" that patrons used to consume their favorite alcoholic beverages. Occasionally, a fight would break out, and the proprietor would caution the other patrons to "Mind your P's & Q's!"

PACIFIC OCEAN

It is the world's largest ocean covering approximately one-third of the earth's surface. It spans over 70 million square miles and its deepest known depth is over 36,000 feet. The name "pacific" means peaceful and was so named by the Portuguese explorer, Ferdinand Magellan.

PALATABLE
(**pal** ut uh ble)

Adj. **Agreeable or pleasing to the taste. Savory.**

• *He had worked hard to prepare a romantic dinner for two, but the meal was barely **palatable**.*

When used to describe an idea or an initiative, etc., it means acceptable, suitable or satisfactory.

• *His plan to reduce our inventories seems **palatable**.*

• *I am afraid that our sales force will not find the changes made to the sales plan very **palatable**.*

PALPABLE
(**pal** puh bul)

Adj. **Readily seen, heard or understood. Obvious. Easily perceived by the senses. Overt or conspicuous.**

• *There were **palpable** errors made throughout the course of the project.*

• *The system we are using to measure employee performance is **palpably** (**adverbial form**) unfair.*

• *A **palpable** error in judgment.*

✪ The opposite of "palpable" is "doubtful" or "uncertain."

PALINDROME
(**pal** in **drome**)

> *Noun.* **A word or phrase that reads the same either backwards or forwards.**
>
> • *Civic. Level. Racecar. Dennis sinned. A Toyota. Madam, I'm Adam. Never odd or even.*

PARADIGM
(**pare** uh **dime**)

> *Noun.* **A model. A pattern. A representative example. A model that forms the basis for a methodology or a theory. A standard. It also defines the current and generally accepted perspective of a particular discipline.**
>
> • *Most scientific disciplines go through a series of **paradigms** as new ideas and technologies are developed.*
>
> • *With the advent of the personal computer, a **paradigmatic** (adjectival form) shift occurred within the computer industry.*

PARADOX
(**pare** uh **docks**)

> *Noun.* **That which is apparently absurd or incredible, but capable of expressing a truth. Seemingly self-contradictory. Ironic. Conflicting with what seems reasonable.**
>
> • *It seems a **paradox** to me that the same group that brought us the storm is now bringing us a plan for safe harbor.*

• *It is a **paradox** how two boorish parents could have such a well-mannered child.*

• *It is a curious **paradox**, but to a point, the faster I read the more information I seem to retain.*

PARAMOUNT
(**pare** uh **mount**)

Adj. **First in importance. Ranking higher than others in consideration or authority. Pre-eminent. Vital.**

• *It is **paramount** that each member of the group has an equal opportunity to express his or her opinion.*

• *The senator reiterated that reducing the budget deficit was of **paramount** importance.*

✪ The opposite of "paramount" is "minor."

PARAPHRASE
(**pare** uh **fraze**)

Noun/Verb. **As a noun it means a free rendering or rewording of something said or written for purposes of clarity or brevity.**

• *He provided us a quick **paraphrase** of what the manager had said.*

As a verb it means to express something in other words. To restate.

• *Since I do not have the directive in front of me, I will **paraphrase** its contents.*

PAROCHIAL
(puh **row** key ul)

> *Adj.* The primary meaning refers to that concerning a parish or parishes. More commonly, the word is used to express that which is narrow, local or limited. Constrained. Restricted in scope. Insular. Confined or localized.
>
> • *His **parochial** views on how to increase sales will not apply to other parts of the country.*
>
> • *Although it is a magazine distributed only in the Southwest, it has managed to keep its editorial views non-**parochial**.*

PARTICIPLE
(**par** tuh **sip** ul)

> *Noun.* Grammatically, it is a word that is formed from verbs and typically functions as an adjective or part of a verb phrase.
>
> The present participle is formed by adding *-ing* to a verb.
>
> • *A talk**ing** parrot.*
>
> The past participle is formed by adding *-ed* to a verb.
>
> • *A learn**ed** professor.*
>
> Do not confuse a present participle with a gerund. While they seem similar, they are different

in syntax. Recall that a gerund is formed by adding–*ing* to a verb, creating a verbal noun while a participle is formed from verbs creating a verbal adjective. Gerunds function as the subject, the direct object, or the object of a preposition in a sentence. This is not the case for a participle.

While participles are formed from verbs, they cannot stand alone as verbs. However, a participle can be used with a helping verb to form a verb phrase.

• *The small baby* **was crying**.

In this instance, the present participle "crying" is considered part of the verb phrase and is not an adjective in the sentence.

A participial phrase is a phrase that consists of a participle and other modifying words that collectively act as an adjective.

• **Sitting at his desk**, *he completed the assignment in record time.*

In this instance, the participial phrase "sitting at his desk" acts as an adjective modifying the pronoun "he."

Usage experts always caution writers on sentences that contain a "dangling participle." Consider the following sentence: "Walking through the supermarket, the bright red apples looked tempting." This is grammatically incorrect since apples cannot walk through a supermarket. You need to ensure that the participial phrase modifies the subject noun. Correct usage would be, "Walking through the supermarket, she thought the bright red apples looked tempting."

PATHOS
(**pay** thos)

Noun. **The quality contained in writing or speech that evokes feelings of sorrow, pity or sadness. That which produces feelings of sympathy for the anguish and misfortunes of others.**

• *It is an enthralling book to read because it contains a significant amount of both humor and **pathos**.*

• *The photographs of the inhabitants of this small village vividly captured the **pathos** of their condition.*

PEREMPTORY
(puh **remp** tuh ree)

Adj. Not allowing refusal or contradiction. Dictatorial. Imperative. Expected to be obeyed immediately and without question. Authoritative. Imperious. That which is final and conclusive.

• *The turn-around expert arrived at the company in full swagger and began immediately to issue **peremptory** instructions.*

• *In a court of law, a lawyer can issue a **peremptory** challenge against any proposed juror without providing a reason. The juror is then released from serving.*

PERENNIAL
(puh **ren** e ul)

> *Adj.* **Lasting a long time. Persistent. Enduring. Everlasting. Continual and recurrent.**
>
> • *He is a **perennial** favorite to win the competition.*
>
> • *Having sufficient funds to meet requisite expenses is a **perennial** problem among most college students.*
>
> **In botanical terms, "perennial" refers to those flowers and shrubs that last for three or more years. Those that die out every year are referred to as annuals.**

PERFUNCTORY
(per **funk** tuh ree)

> *Adj.* **Performing some function simply to discharge the responsibility. Done with no concerted effort or interest. Mechanical. Automatically done.**
>
> • *As we entered the door, she gave us a **perfunctory** greeting.*
>
> • *As the two senators emerged from the meeting, they posed **perfunctorily** (**adverbial form**) for the news photographers.*

PERIPHERAL
(puh **riff** er ul)

> *Adj.* **Of little importance. Marginal. Nonessential. Minor or secondary. Tangential. Something**

relatively unimportant or of lesser importance than something else.

• *We receive* ***peripheral*** *support from their department.*

• *The novel includes far too much* ***peripheral*** *detail that is neither interesting nor supportive of the story line.*

It also describes equipment used with a computer, but not an essential part of its function.

• *We ordered additional* ***peripheral*** *computer equipment.*

Do not confuse "peripheral" with "periphery" (puh **riff** a ree). "Periphery" is a noun that means the outside boundary or limits of an area.

• *The new stadium will be constructed on property located on the* ***periphery*** *of the city.*

PERTINENT
(**purr** tuh nent)

Adj. Pertaining to the matter or situation at hand. Fitting. That which is relevant or applicable. Apposite.

• *We need all of the* ***pertinent*** *details before we can create an action plan.*

• *His comments were not* ***pertinent*** *to our discussion.*

PERUSE
(puh **rooze**)

> *Verb.* **To read carefully. To scrutinize. To read or study in detail. To examine.**
>
> • *He asked each of the managers to **peruse** the recommended plan and then submit his or her ideas and suggestions.*
>
> • *The teacher **perused** the student's essay carefully, but could find no egregious or glaring errors.*

✪   The opposite of "peruse" is "skim," or "scan."

PERVASIVE
(purr **vay** siv)

> *Adj.* **That which has extended its influence widely. Spreading and saturating throughout. Existing everywhere.**
>
> • *He was concerned over the **pervasive** nature of the rumor.*
>
> • *Most feel we brought the software to market too early, and as a result, the notion is **pervasive** within our sales ranks that the software is too bug-laden.*
>
> • *Guns and drugs are major contributors to the violence that **pervades** (**verb form**) our country.*

PHILHARMONIC
(**fill** har **mon** ik)

> *Adj.* **The word simply means fond of music. Music-loving. Typically used in the names of various musical societies and orchestras.**

> • *The Boston **Philharmonic.***

> • *The New York **Philharmonic**-Symphony Orchestra*

PLACATE
(**play kate**)

> *Verb.* **To pacify. To calm. To appease or soothe. To conciliate. To mollify.**

> • *The store manager was called in to **placate** the angry customer.*

> • *The furor his original theories created was finally **placated** when he released further supporting evidence that validated his assumptions.*

PLACID
(**plas** id)

> *Adj.* **Calm. Composed. Not easily aroused. Un-flustered or relaxed. Not easily disturbed by emotion.**

> • *A large sand bar protected the **placid** bay from the surging currents of the ocean.*

> • *Although he had a great deal of money at risk, he maintained a **placid** disposition throughout the entire ordeal.*

PLAINTIFF
(**plain** tiff)

> A claimant. A petitioner. One who files suit in a court of law. On the other hand, the individual being sued is called the defendant.

PLAINTIVE
(**plain** tiv)

> *Adj.* Expressing sadness or sorrow. Lamenting. Melancholic. Mournful.

> • *The unhappy news brought a **plaintive** expression to his face.*

> • *He had now been in the war-torn country for two years and the letters to his parents became increasingly **plaintive**.*

PLATITUDE
(**plat** uh tude)

> *Noun.* A trite remark. A tired and worn out expression. A cliché. Especially one solemnly delivered as though it were new or profound.

> • *"Plan your work and work your plan."*

> • *"If at first you don't succeed, try, try again."*

> • *"Curiosity killed the cat."*

POCKET VETO

> When congress passes a bill, it is then sent to the President of the United States for signature. If the

bill is presented within 10 days prior to adjournment and the President simply retains the bill without signing it, it is the equivalent of a veto.

PONDEROUS
(**pon** der us)

Adj. There are two major definitions of this word. First, it means something of great weight. Heavy. Bulky. Massive or cumbersome.

• *A **ponderous** mass of granite was required to construct the building.*

Secondly, when referring to something written, it means dull, tedious, wearisome, or mind numbing.

• *No one was pleased at having to read such a **ponderous** essay.*

POWER OF ATTORNEY
(Law) A legal document given by one person to another vesting the latter with the authority to act for the former.

PORTENTOUS
(por **ten** tus)

Adj. Ominous. Indicating something momentous is about to happen. Something presaged or prophetic. Indicating a future event.

• *The dark clouds circling above us seemed to be a **portentous** indication of what we could expect.*

• *It is distressing to think that many* **portentous** *recommendations had been made in the past on the need to establish a tsunami early warning system in the Indian Ocean.*

Don't confuse "portentous" with the adjective "pretentious" (pre ten shus). "Pretentious" means showy, ostentatious, pompous, full of self-importance.

• *He had many degrees, awards, photographs and certificates hanging in his office. They appeared to be a* **pretentious** *display of his accomplishments.*

PRAGMATIC
(prag **mat** ik)
> *Adj.* **Practical. Being realistic and sensible. Levelheaded and down-to-earth.**

> • *A more* **pragmatic** *approach to teaching is to combine theoretical classroom instruction with real hands-on experiences.*

> • *His approach to life was simple and* **pragmatic***; you have to take the good with the bad.*

✪   The opposite of "pragmatic" is "idealistic."

PRECIPITATE
(pre **sip** uh **tate** [tit])
> *Noun/Verb/Adj.* **This is an unusually flexible word because it is properly and commonly used as a noun, a verb, or an adjective. As a noun: "Precipitate" (pronounced pre sip uh tit) can**

mean that which has been separated from a solution by a chemical process. It also refers to moisture that has been condensed into rain or dew.

• *The area received over two inches of* ***precipitate****.*

As a verb: "Precipitate" (pronounced pre **sip** uh tate) means to hasten an occurrence. To cause something to happen prematurely. To quicken.

• *The notion that weapons of mass destruction were being developed was one of the elements that* ***precipitated*** *the war against Iraq.*

As an adjective: "Precipitate" (pronounced pre **sip** uh tit) means proceeding or going onward with speed and rapidity. Something done in haste.

• *Once they recognized the superiority of the opposing forces, the small patrol made a* ***precipitate*** *departure.*

PRECLUDE
(pre **klude**)
> *Verb.* To prevent. To stop. To prohibit an occurrence. To exclude or shut out.

• *The new guidelines* ***preclude*** *us from submitting our forecasts via the mail. Now, everything must be sent online.*

• *His employment contract* ***precludes*** *him from accepting employment with a competitive firm until two years after termination.*

• *Those who have not achieved 100% of their assigned objectives will be **precluded** from attending the awards ceremony.*

• *The new city council resolution **precluded** smoking in public places.*

✪   The opposite of "preclude" is "permit."

PRECONCEPTION
(pre kun **sep** shun)

>*Noun.* **A notion or belief already formed. A previously conceived idea. A bias or prejudice. Already predisposed.**

• *The group had the **preconception** that the subject matter would be difficult to understand.*

• *She had a **preconceived** (**adjectival form**) notion that any training session utilizing closed circuit television would be embarrassing.*

PRECURSOR
(pre **kur** ser)

>*Noun.* **A forerunner. That which precedes another. A predecessor. That which comes before. An antecedent event or thing.**

• *The harpsichord is the **precursor** of the piano.*

PREEMINENT
(pre **em** uh nent)

>*Adj.* **Distinguished. Excelling above all others. Unsurpassed. Superior in quality and reputation.**

• *The professor occupies a* **preeminent** *position in the field of quantum mechanics.*

• *To this point, what has not been challenged is the United States'* **preeminence** (**noun form**) *in space exploration.*

PREVALENT
(**prev** uh lent)

Adj. **Widespread. Commonplace. Existing generally. Prevailing. Commonly occurring.**

• *The notion of equal pay for equal work is not as* **prevalent** *as one would hope.*

• *It is a sad commentary on our society, but strong feelings of helplessness and loneliness are* **prevalent** *among the elderly.*

✪   The opposite of "prevalent" is "rare."

PRINCIPAL
(**prin** suh pul)

Noun/Adj. **The word means high in rank or importance. Major. Chief or foremost.**

AUTHOR'S NOTE
Learn the difference between "principal" and "principle." Here are some examples of how "principal" is used as both a noun and an adjective.

155

- The **principal**—*presiding officer of a school.*

- **Principal** *cause—the foremost reason of some action.*

- **Principal** *sum—interest is paid on this amount.*

- **Principal** *actor—the leading performer.*

- *A **principal**—someone with an agent acting on his or her behalf. Also, a key person in an organization.*

- **Principal** *clause—the main clause in a sentence.*

PRINCIPLE
(**prin** suh pul)

Noun. **A fundamental belief. A rule of conduct. A fundamental truth. That which provides guiding influence on our behavior.**

- *His parents had taught him at an early age the basic **principles** that guided his life.*

- *She was a woman of **principle** and integrity.*

AUTHOR'S NOTE
Since there are many and more varied uses of the word "principal" versus "principle," if you are in doubt as to which word to use—call on your *(pal).*

PRISTINE
(pris **teen**)

>*Adj.* **Pure. Spotless. Manifesting its original purity. Unspoiled. Immaculately clean.**
>
>• *There is a danger in having too **pristine** an approach to our presentation. We should include information on the weaknesses of our competitor's products and let the customer make an informed decision.*
>
>• *The crest of the mountain was covered with **pristine**, white snow.*

PROBITY
(**pro** buh tee)

>*Noun.* **Decency. Honesty. Integrity. Moral excellence. Unimpeachable virtue.**
>
>• *He was a principled individual who lived his life with a high regard for moral correctness and **probity**.*
>
>• *Until financial **probity** is restored, no serious investor will have confidence in the viability of this company.*
>
>• *His integrity and **probity** are exemplary and beyond question.*

❂   The opposite of "probity" is "wickedness."

PROBLEMATIC
(**prob** luh **mat** ik)

>*Adj.* **Also "problematical," but "problematic" is preferred. Representing or posing a problem.**

That which is difficult or challenging. Having the nature of uncertainty and doubt. Questionable. Puzzling. Hard to comprehend or solve. Not definite.

• *Because we were given the assignment with little or no guidelines, finding the solution became* **problematic**.

• *With little or no resources and no college degree, his future remains* **problematic**.

PROCLIVITY
(pro **kliv** uh tee)
Noun. **An inclination. A tendency. A leaning toward. An affinity to. A penchant.**

• *No one liked being around him since he had a* **proclivity** *to find fault with almost everything.*

• *He has a* **proclivity** *for fine wines and exquisite meals.*

PRODIGY
(**prod** uh gee)
Noun. **One outside of the normal course of nature. A person gifted or endowed with special talents, especially a child. Having exceptional abilities.**

• *Mozart was a child* **prodigy** *who learned to play the harpsichord at age three and was composing music at age five.*

PROFUSELY
(pro **fuse** lee)

> *Adv.* **Abundantly. Generously. Copiously. Freely and extravagantly. In large amounts.**
>
> • *She was **profusely** generous in her charitable contributions.*
>
> • *He apologized **profusely** for failing to remember her birthday.*
>
> • *You have to marvel at the **profusion** (**noun form**) of information available on the Internet.*

✪　　The opposite of "profusely" is "meagerly."

PROLETARIAT
(**pro** luh **tare** e ut)

> **The working class. The class without property. Those without capital. Those who support themselves on daily or part time employment.**

PROLIFIC
(pro **lif** ik)

> *Adj.* **The capacity to produce many offspring. The capacity to produce significant output. Fertile. Fruitful. Abundantly productive.**
>
> • *We took an excursion through Bordeaux, France, to visit some of the most **prolific** wine vineyards in the world.*
>
> • *John O'Hara was a **prolific** writer.*

Author's note
Stephen King, with over 35 books to his credit, is also considered a prolific writer. In his revealing and insightful book, *On Writing: A Memoir of the Craft,* King relates that the Secretariat of prolific writing is British mystery writer, John Creasey, who during his lifetime produced over 500 novels under ten different names.

PROMULGATE
(**prom** ul **gate**)

Verb. To announce. To make known to the public. To spread or circulate. To publicize. To proclaim formally.

• *Each real estate agent should use only those forms* **promulgated** *by the real estate commission.*

The word "promulgate" implies some sort of regulatory control and should not be confused with or used interchangeably with the verb "disseminate" (deh **sim** uh **nate**), which means to scatter about or to spread widely. To give out.

• *The Human Resources Department will be* **disseminating** *the information to all employees*

PROPHETIC
(pro **fet** ik)

Adj. Its primary meaning is pertaining to a prophet. More commonly, the word is used to describe something visionary or farsighted. Predictive or foretelling of future events.

• *Because of the subsequent events that transpired, his* **prophetic** *advice to withhold funding has saved the company a great deal of money.*

• *Much of what he had written on the future of the Middle East appears to be grimly* **prophetic**.

Two forms of this word have caused writers problems, mainly because they are pronounced the same but spelled differently. The word "prophecy" (**prof** uh see) is the noun form and is a statement of what will happen in the future. A prediction. A foretelling. Religiously, a prediction made as a result of divine revelation.

• *Throughout the history of mankind, people have sought knowledge of future events from those individuals who were considered to have the gift of* **prophecy**.

The word "prophesy" (**prof** uh see) is the verb form of this word and is the act of stating what you believe will happen in the future. Foretelling what the future holds.

• *Despite questioning from the press, he refused to* **prophesy** *the governor's chances for re-election.*

• *There are few who could have* **prophesied** *the total destruction and carnage caused by Hurricane Katrina.*

PROPRIETARY
(pruh **pry** uh teri)

> *Adj.* **Relating to an owner. Relating to a proprietor. Characteristic of ownership. It is more commonly used to indicate exclusive rights of an individual or corporation that has manufactured a product that is being sold in the marketplace. These rights include patents, logos, trademarks, formulas, etc. that the marketplace identifies with the product.**

> • *Microsoft's **proprietary** software.*

PROSAIC
(pro **zae** ik)

> *Adj.* **Dull and unimaginative. Mundane. Commonplace. Uninteresting and unexciting.**

> • *Your sales materials lack punch and excitement. It almost seems too **prosaic** an approach to be effective.*

> • *While it had a few interesting moments, it was basically a **prosaic** play that was panned by the critics.*

AUTHOR'S NOTE
The word is derived from the word "prose," meaning ordinary prose as compared to the artistic quality of lyrical poetry.

PROSCRIBE
(pro **scribe**)

> *Verb.* **To denounce or condemn. To forbid. To**

prohibit by those in authority. To make illegal. To limit or banish. To ban.

• *The city council passed a resolution that **proscribes** smoking in all public places.*

• *In athletics, the governing body of most organizations **proscribes** the use of certain drugs by those participating in the events.*

"Proscribe" is oftentimes confused with the word "prescribe" (pre scribe). "Prescribe" is a verb meaning to provide a course of action to be followed. To give counsel or designate. Thus, a prescribed drug is one provided at the request of a medical person as a remedy for a specific ailment, while a proscribed drug is one that has been banned. As you might expect, certain prescribed drugs have been proscribed in various athletic events.

PROTRACT
(pro trackt)

Verb. To extend or draw out. To prolong or extend in time. To lengthen in duration.

• *The danger of adding more people to the committee is that it may only serve to **protract** the amount of time it will take to make decisions.*

• *The lack of supplies and troops in the northern region **protracted** the war by three months.*

• *The **protracted** (past participle) negotiations made everyone weary.*

PRUDENT
(**pru** dent)

> *Adj.* **Judicious. Careful and wise in practical affairs. Discreet. Carefully considered. Circumspect. Showing sensible self-restraint in actions and speech.**

> • *She decided it was more **prudent** to turn the other cheek than to cause a scene.*

> • *He **prudently** (**adverbial form**) reviewed all of the data from each of the manufacturers before making his final decision.*

> ✪   The opposite of "prudent" is "reckless."

PSEUDO-
(**sue** doe)

> **A word element meaning "false."**

PSEUDONYM
(**sue** duh nim)

> *Noun.* **A false or assumed name. A pen name.**

• *Mark Twain is a **pseudonym** for Samuel Langhorne Clemens (1835–1910), American author and humorist.*

PURVIEW
(**purr** view)
> *Noun.* **The scope or range of operation. The range of physical or mental vision. The range of concern or responsibility.**

> • *These responsibilities should fall under the **purview** of our field managers.*

> • *Personnel issues such as these come under the **purview** of the Human Resources Manager.*

PURGE
(**purrj**)
> *Verb.* **To cleanse. To get rid of whatever is undesirable. To flush out or wash out. To remove or do away with.**

> • *His first action as the new manager was to **purge** the organization of under-performing employees.*

> • *The initial draft was **purged** of all foul and offensive language.*

> • *The party leaders summarily **purged** fanatical extremists from their political ranks.*

PYRRHIC VICTORY
(**peer** ik)

A victory achieved at such a high cost that it is of little value to the victor. So named for Pyrrhus, King of Epirus. After conquering the Romans, he sustained such heavy losses that it rendered his army ineffective.

• *The U. S. Olympic Basketball Team may have registered a* **Pyrrhic victory** *in their first round win over Germany. Three of the starters were injured in the game and appear to be out for the remainder of the Olympic Games.*

QUAGMIRE
(**kwag** mire)

Noun. A marsh. A swamp. Boggy ground. The more common use of the word is metaphoric. It means a situation that is difficult to get free of or to extract yourself from. A dilemma. A predicament. A quandary. A precarious situation.

• *As early radio sportscasters were fond of saying, "The game was played in a virtual* **quagmire.**"

• *The script called for the actor to be immersed in a* **quagmire** *of deceit, murder and intrigue.*

QUALM
(**kwalm**)

Noun. A misgiving. A feeling of apprehensiveness. Doubt as to conduct. A feeling of uneasiness. Doubt that you are doing the right thing.

• *Because he had been with the firm for so long, she had serious* **qualms** *about removing him from his position.*

• *The sales manager held separate meetings with those individuals who seemingly had no* **qualms** *about submitting sales forecasts significantly higher than anything they had ever achieved before.*

QUASIMODO
(**qua** zee **mow** doe)

> The name of the hunchback of Notre Dame. It is from Victor Hugo's classic novel, *Notre Dame de Paris*.

QUELL
(**kwel**)

> *Verb.* To put down or repress. To subdue. To inhibit further action. To suppress some strong emotion.

• *By nightfall, the military police had* **quelled** *the rebellious group.*

• *The sumptuous meal* **quelled** *his appetite.*

• *The latest financial disclosures did little to* **quell** *the growing concern among the employees over the company's viability and future.*

QUINTESSENTIAL
(**kwin** tuh **sin** shul)

> *Adj.* The essence of something. The embodiment or personification of some quality. The perfect example or ideal.

• *Because of his talents and years of experience, many consider him the* **quintessential** *Broadway actor.*

• *Ludwig van Beethoven is widely regarded as the* **quintessential** *symphonic composer.*

> ### AUTHOR'S NOTE
> Beethoven's Symphony No. 5 is probably the most well-known and popular classical composition of all time. It is easily recognized by its four-note opening that resembles the letter "V" in the Morse Code (dot dot dot dash). The British Broadcasting Company during WWII used those notes to open their radio broadcasts as an indication of "victory."

QUIXOTIC
(quicks **ot** ik)

Adj. **Absurdly romantic and excessively chivalrous. Foolishly impractical. Fanciful. Idealistic in the pursuit of lofty goals. Highly imaginative, but not practical. Starry-eyed.**

• *While we were all amused at what he had recommended, his* **quixotic** *approach on how to hire new employees was far too impractical.*

• *To many Americans at the time, the proposed manned space flight program seemed to be a* **quixotic** *endeavor that was far too expensive and not likely to succeed.*

> **AUTHOR'S NOTE**
> This is a word that has passed into the English language as a result of a widely read satirical account of chivalric romances written by Miguel Cervantes. It is entitled *Don Quixote* (key **hoe** tee) and tells the story of an affable knight who believes he must travel the world in search of high adventure and romance.

✪   The opposite of "quixotic" is "down-to-earth."

RACONTEUR
(**rack** on **tour**)
> *Noun.* **A storyteller. One skilled at telling stories and anecdotes.**
>
> • *Many believe that Garrison Keillor is today's most entertaining and interesting **raconteur**.*

> **AUTHOR'S NOTE**
> An anecdote is a short, interesting story about a particular person, place or event.

RANCOROUS
(**rang** ker us)
> *Adj.* **Full of bitterness. Displaying malignant hatred. Resentful. Acrimonious. Deep seated ill will.**

• *The last meeting between the company's senior officials was full of **rancorous** debate.*

• *The politics surrounding embryonic stem cell research has evolved from differences of opinion to one of **rancorous** dissent.*

• *It was refreshing to see them resolve their dispute without **rancor** (**noun form**).*

RAPACIOUS
(ruh **pay** shus)
> *Adj.* **Grasping. Gluttonous. Greedy. Over-reaching. Somewhat predatory in nature. Voracious. Ravenous.**

• *Even at an early age, the child showed a **rapacious** appetite for books.*

• *He was an aggressive and **rapacious** businessman who had achieved great wealth even though some consider his methods somewhat questionable.*

RARITY
(**rare** uh tee)
> *Noun.* **Something that is rare or uncommon. Infrequency. That which is valued for being rare or scarce. Exceptional.**

• *It is a **rarity** to see someone so young behave with such maturity and poise.*

• *She is a **rarity** among our sales force because she combines excellent technical abilities with impressive selling skills.*

RATIONALE
(**rash** uh **nowl**)

> *Noun.* **An underlying principle. A consolidated statement of reasons. The foundation or logical basis of anything. An explanation of controlling beliefs.**
>
> • *It is difficult to completely understand the* **rationale** *behind their actions.*
>
> • *There are many who would argue against the* **rationale** *for capital punishment.*

RE-

> **A prefix meaning "again," "once more," or "anew." It can be attached to many verbs like "act" or "adjust" to form "react" and "readjust." Remember, however, when this prefix is attached to a verb that begins with "e," a hyphen is required.**
>
> • *Re-elect. Re-enter. Re-enact. Re-enlist.*
>
> **Also know that if the addition of "re" to a verb spells an existing word then a hyphen is also required.**
>
> • *If you wanted to cover something again, you could not use the word "***recover.***" The word " recover" could mean to recover from an illness. Proper usage would be* **re**-*cover.*

REALISM
(**real** ism)
> The practice or belief of dealing only with that which is real or actual. Regarding things in their true nature as compared to abstract notions. In art and literature it means an adherence to treating life as it is as opposed to idealism.

REALTY
(**real** tee)
> It simply means real property. Real estate.

REANIMATE
(ree **an** uh **mate**)
> *Verb.* To bring back to life. To restore or to resuscitate. To give new vigor or spirit. To stimulate.

> • *The manager expected the training session to **reanimate** the sales division's marketing activities.*

> • *She moved with a model's easy grace and had an orthodontic masterpiece for a smile. His languid spirits were promptly **reanimated**.*

REASONLESS
(**ree** zen lus)
> *Adj.* Without reason. Groundless. Absence of logic. With no rationale.

> • *His actions and words were a **reasonless** display of anger.*

> • *It is mind numbing to think that you could have arrived at such a **reasonless** decision.*

RECALCITRANT
(ree **cal** suh trunt)

Adj. **Resisting authority. Defying control. Disobedient. Refractory. Not compliant. Obstinate.**

• *Our organization will simply not condone such recalcitrant behavior.*

• *His genius was in his recalcitrant approach to eschewing established methods and procedures.*

• *In due course, the university suspended the most recalcitrant of the demonstrators.*

RECANT
(ree **cant**)

Verb. **To retract. To take back. To disavow. To renounce something said or done previously.**

• *Because the developments of the past few days brought new information to bear, he was forced to recant his previous statements.*

• *The governor issued a press release stating he would not recant his position on the state's laws governing the death penalty.*

RECIPROCAL
(ree **sip** ruh cul)

Adj. **Something given for something in return. A mutual interchange. An exchange. Characteristic of reciprocity.**

- *The two companies signed **reciprocal** licensing agreements allowing each to market the other's products.*

- *Unfortunately, my feelings for her were not **reciprocated** (verb form).*

- *They spent Christmas with us last year, and this year we are going to **reciprocate**.*

RECOLLECTION
(**rek** uh **lek** shun)
> *Noun.* **Something remembered. Something called to mind. The act of recalling or remembering.**

- *I believe a **recollection** by all concerned will verify my statements.*

- *We played a card game called Concentration all through college, and he rarely lost a game because his powers of **recollection** were so phenomenal.*

RECONCILE
(**rek** un **sile**)
> *Verb.* **To settle or resolve. To bring into agreement. To make compatible. To no longer differ or oppose.**

- *We are having great difficulty **reconciling** your point of view with the facts.*

- *In the past, she **reconciled** her checking account as soon as the monthly statement arrived from the bank. Now, she does it on-line.*

• *After discussing the matter for over an hour, they were able to* **reconcile** *their differences.*

RECONDITE
(**rek** un **dite**)

Adj. **Difficult to understand. Abstruse. Complex or obscure. Hard to comprehend. Profound.**

• *The main subject matter of this course covers the* **recondite** *principles and theories of statistical analysis.*

• *He was a writer's writer—sometimes* **recondite**, *sometimes simplistic—but he never lost sight of the need to tell a good story.*

RECTITUDE
(**rek** tuh **tude**)

Noun. **Righteousness. Correctness of purpose. Rightness of principle. Moral uprightness.**

• *Because of the enormous benefits that could be derived, no one questioned the* **rectitude** *of her undertaking.*

• *In his political position, he wielded enormous power and influence, but nevertheless remained a man of unquestioned moral* **rectitude**.

RECURRENT
(ree **kur** ent)

Adj. **Happening repeatedly or frequently. Persistent and ongoing. Happening again and again.**

• *His absence from our sessions is a* **recurrent** *problem.*

• *The romance and grandeur of the old West is a **recurrent** theme in most of his novels.*

• *Although he sought medical attention frequently, for most of his life he suffered from **recurrent** bouts of depression.*

REDOUBTABLE
(ree **dow** tuh bul)

Adj. **Formidable. Powerful. Exhibiting forceful ability. Something to be feared. Something that commands respect.**

• *We have a **redoubtable** opponent; let's be prepared.*

• *Without question, he is a **redoubtable** challenger for the heavyweight title.*

• *A consensus of PGA players will confirm that today there is none on tour more skilled and **redoubtable** than Tiger Woods.*

✪   The opposite of "redoubtable" is "weak," "powerless," or "impotent."

REDRESS
(ree **dress**)

Noun/Verb. **As a noun it means that which is provided to rectify a wrongdoing or a grievance. A remedy. A cure.**

• *There are always a few who will complain without justification, but there is occasion for **redress** when the grumbling is universal.*

As a verb it means to set right what is wrong. . To set straight again. To correct a harmful situation. To mend or resolve.

• *It is imperative that we **redress** the inequitable distribution of quota that has been assigned to our sales force.*

REDUNDANT
(ree **dun** dunt)

Adj. **That which can be omitted without loss of understanding or significance. Unnecessary. In excess. Superfluous. Nonessential.**

• *The following phrases are **redundant**:*

  • A free gift

  • A convicted felon

  • An advance warning

AUTHOR'S NOTE

In most instances, being redundant is something you want to avoid. This is especially true in expository prose where the reader can become annoyed or exhausted when the writer feels compelled to expand or overemphasize the various points he is trying to make. Tighten up your paragraph construction by eliminating those unneeded and nonessential phrases and your writing will become more clear and concise. Formal studies have proven that your reader will not only better understand what you are presenting, but will retain the information for a longer period of time.

Keep in mind, however, that many complex systems such as computers or airplanes have redundant systems within the design architecture that will activate if the primary systems fail. While they are unneeded as long as the primary systems are operative, they are a necessary part of the overall design.

REFLUX
(ree fluks)

Noun. **A backward flow. A returning motion. An ebb. A rearward surge.**

• *He suffered from an abnormal **reflux** of stomach fluids.*

• *The new and more stringent guidelines that required*

additional information gathering and reporting prompted an instant **reflux** *of dissatisfaction from the Administration Division.*

REFURBISH
(ree **fur** bish)

Verb. **To renew. To renovate. To polish up or make new again. To restore or redecorate.**

• *Provisions within the lease stipulate that at the end of the primary term, the tenant would have the right to renew for another five-year term, and the landlord would be required to* **refurbish** *the offices at no cost to the tenant.*

• *Every room in the house underwent a* **refurbishment** **(noun form).**

• *They were simply old ideas and principles* **refurbished** *with new information gained from current testing and experimentation.*

REGRESS
(ree **gress**)

Verb. **To go back. To move in a backward motion. To return to a former state or condition. To revert back.**

• *It is very sad and heart-rending, but patients with this disease typically* **regress** *mentally to the level of a young child.*

• *Late in the season, the team seemed to* **regress** *to its* *early season habit of making foolish mistakes at inopportune times.*

REJOINDER
(ree **join** dur)
> *Noun.* **A reply. What is said in answer to a question. A retort. A response.**
>
> • *One can only smile at the classic* **rejoinder** *of the infamous bank robber, Willie Sutton, when asked why he robbed banks. He replied, "Because, that's where the money is."*
>
> • *As we approached, the sales clerk dutifully asked, "May I help you?" To which my friend promptly* **rejoined,** **(verb form)** *"I am afraid we're beyond help."*

RELINQUISH
(ree **link** quish)
> *Verb.* **To surrender or give up a right or possession. To hand over. To let go or put aside. To abandon. To forgo.**
>
> • *Because of his lengthy illness, he* **relinquished** *all hope of completing the project on time.*
>
> • *By marrying a commoner, she* **relinquished** *her claim to the throne.*

REMBRANDT
(1606–1669) A highly prolific Dutch painter whose output included religious themes, landscape paintings, drawings and etchings. He is

most noted for having created over 60 self-portraits, an extended effort in either self-love or self-analysis.

REMEDIAL
(ruh **me** de ul)

Adj. **Corrective. Intended as a remedy. Curative. Restorative. That which is intended to rectify or improve. That which removes or abates what is dismal or ineffective.**

• *With health and welfare its primary focus, the World Health Organization has initiated several* **remedial** *programs.*

• ***Remedial*** reading courses were offered to those students whose scores were sub-standard.

• *The vice president of Sales advised the field managers to initiate* **remedial** *training sessions for those who were underachieving.*

REMISS
(ree **miss**)

Adj. **Careless. Inattentive to obligations. Lax in duty and responsibility. Negligent or thoughtless. Lacking earnestness.**

• *I would be* **remiss** *if I did not thank all of the volunteers who worked so tirelessly to make this event a success.*

• *There are many who feel government officials have*

*been **remiss** in warning all Americans of the potential dangers of hepatitis C, a virus that infects millions and kills thousands every year.*

REPARTEE
(**rep** ar **tee**)

> *Noun.* **A quick and clever reply. A response that is witty. A clever and sharp retort. Skillful banter.**
>
> • *When the two of them got together, the ensuing **repartee** amused everyone.*
>
> • *He was a widely acclaimed playwright whose plays were full of witty **repartee**.*

REPREHENSIBLE
(**rep** ree **hen** suh bul)

> *Adj.* **Blameworthy. In the wrong. That which could be rebuked or censured. At fault. Culpable.**
>
> • *His childish behavior is **reprehensible** because it sets such a bad example for the new employees.*
>
> • *The most glaring and perhaps most **reprehensible** aspect of the essay was its narrow-minded intolerance of other opinions.*
>
> ✪   The opposite of "reprehensible" is "innocent."

REPUDIATE
(ree **pew** dee **ate**)

> *Verb.* **This is a versatile word that basically means**

"to reject," but there are certain subtleties to its meaning depending on what is being rejected.

• *If you* **repudiate** *a claim, you are rejecting either the binding force of the claim or the entity (authority) that issued the claim.*

• *If you* **repudiate** *a son or daughter, you are denying or disowning the child.*

• *If you* **repudiate** *certain religious doctrine, you disapprove or condemn its principles.*

• *If you* **repudiate** *a debt, you are refusing to acknowledge the validity of the debt.*

REQUISITE
(**rek** wuh zit)

Adj. **That which is necessary. That which is required by circumstance. Indispensable. Essential. Required.**

• *She has demonstrated all of the* **requisite** *qualifications to fill the position.*

• *It is our duty and responsibility to provide all employees with the* **requisite** *tools necessary to do their jobs.*

RESCIND
(ree **send**)

Verb. **To cancel. To revoke. To repeal or terminate. To withdraw. To reverse a previous condition. To make void.**

• *After further study and consideration, the president* **rescinded** *his approval of the expenditure.*

• *The purchase agreement contains a provision that if the stock price rises above $20 per share, the offer will be* **rescinded***.*

• *There are many who believe it is just a matter of time before Congress will vote to* **rescind** *the embargo on trade with Cuba.*

While the pronunciations are similar, do not confuse "rescind" with "resend," which simply means to send something again.

RESILIENT
(ree **zil** e ent)

Adj. **Rebounding quickly. Returning to its original shape after bending or stretching. Easily recoiled. Swiftly recovering from some negative event.**

• *One of the significant characteristics of a true sales professional is the ability to maintain a* **resilient** *nature in the face of marketplace rejections.*

• *Rather than feeling victimized or depressed,* **resilient** *individuals have the uncanny ability to successfully cope with the various misfortunes that enter their lives.*

RESOLUTE
(**rez** uh **loot**)

Adj. **Firm of purpose. Determined. Staunch and**

unyielding. Steadfast. Unwavering and unfalter-
ing. Undaunted. Adamant.

• *He had a* **resolute** *desire to reach the highest levels of
management within the firm.*

• *She* **resolutely** **(adverbial form)** *denied any participation in the demonstration.*

• *In the face of* **resolute** *opposition, he acquiesced to
their demands.*

RETICENT
(**ret** uh cent)

Adj. **Reserved. Quiet. Not inclined to speak
openly and freely. Uncommunicative. Taciturn.
Remaining silent.**

• *We would have learned more about the incident, but
she remained* **reticent** *throughout most of the investigation.*

• *For the first few days of the class, the students appeared*
reticent *and unwilling to participate in open discus-
sions.*

The noun form of "reticent" is "reticence" (ret a
sense)**, which is the state or condition of being
non-communicative.**

• *His* **reticence** *to discuss his background made us sus-
picious.*

✪   The opposite of "reticent" is "talkative."

RETRENCH
(ree **trench**)
> *Verb.* To cut back. To economize. To limit or make cuts. To reduce the amount of.

> • *Because sales were down, the company was forced to* **retrench** *by closing field offices and terminating a portion of their work force.*

> **The noun form of this word is "retrenchment"** (ree **trench** ment). **It is mostly a military term that means a second line of defense interior to the front line that would be available to retreating front line troops.**

RETRO-
(**ret** ro)
> **A prefix meaning "backwards" in space or time.**

RETROSPECT
(**ret** ro **spekt**)
> *Noun.* **A reference or contemplation of the past. A review of past events. Hindsight. A consideration of what has taken place beforehand.**

> • *In* **retrospect**, *our time would have been better spent developing new products rather than attempting to upgrade our existing line.*

> • *The essay is an interesting and informative* **retrospective** (noun form) *on the life and times of author John Steinbeck.*

• *The purpose of this meeting is not to be* **retrospective** **(adjectival form)**, *but to determine what new strategy we can employ going forward that will enhance our chances of success.*

REVOKE
(ree **voke**)

Verb. **To cancel. To withdraw. To repeal or invalidate. To rescind. To reverse or take back.**

• *Because of his appalling driving record, the state* **revoked** *his driver's license.*

• *The zoning commission* **revoked** *their original decision that granted permission to develop an office building on the site.*

• *A* **revocable** **(adjectival form)** *trust is one that can be changed depending on the needs of the beneficiaries. An irrevocable trust cannot be changed, altered or annulled.*

RHETORICAL QUESTION
Noun. **A question asked when no answer is expected or given. It is asked for dramatic effect only.**

• *"Who cares?" is a* **rhetorical question** *when everyone knows no one cares.*

R.S.V.P.
(French) *Répondez S'il Vous Plaît.* **"Please Respond."**

SAGACIOUS
(suh **gay** shus)

> *Adj.* **Keenly perceptive. Wise. Astute. Having practical wisdom. Insightful. Discerning. Of keen judgment. Sage. Shrewd.**
>
> • *Being a **sagacious** judge of character is one of the reasons for his success.*
>
> • *She is much too insightful and **sagacious** to be taken in by such specious arguments.*

SALIENT
(**say** lee ent)

> *Adj.* **Most important. Prominent. Significant or conspicuous. Foremost.**
>
> • *He was asked to peruse the entire report and then provide us with a summary of the **salient** points.*
>
> • *The mediator was given a report on the **salient** facts surrounding the dispute.*

SANTA FE TRAIL

> **A significant trading route beginning in Independence, Missouri, and extending approximately 780 miles to Santa Fe, New Mexico. It was used by traders and suppliers to transport goods and supplies into the area. The trail was abandoned in 1880 when the Santa Fe Railroad reached Santa Fe.**

SAPLESS
(**sap** lis)

> *Adj.* The primary meaning of this word is devoid of sap. Withered or dried out. More common usage is as a reference to something that lacks vitality. Infirm. Something that is dull or insipid. Uninspired. Weak.

> • *It was a book that employed a much used and worn-out theme—a* **sapless** *account of a young man coming of age in the 1960s.*

> • *Returning home, she appeared* **sapless** *from the exhausting events of the day.*

SARDONIC
(sar **don** ik)

> *Adj.* Sarcastic. Scornful. Disdainfully humorous. That which is mocking or sneering. Mordant. Being unkind in a humorous way.

> • *She was not sorry to see him go. Certainly, she would not miss the* **sardonic** *smile that seemed permanently plastered on his face.*

> • *She felt intimidated by his biting,* **sardonic** *comments.*

SATIRE
(**sat tire**)

> *Noun.* A spoof. A lampoon. That which makes fun of or ridicules. A literary technique of either verse or prose that attempts to hold human weak-

nesses, vices or shortcomings up for ridicule or scorn. Morality and virtue are always on the side of the satirists. They use humor in an attempt to change or uncover human frailties.

• *Certain sketches on the television show, "Saturday Night Live," and Sinclair Lewis's novel,* Elmer Gantry, *are examples of* **satire**.

• *The comic strip "Doonesbury" once* **satirized** **(verb form)** *a Florida county that had a law requiring minorities to have written permission to be in a particularly affluent area of the county. The law was later rescinded by an act that became known as the Doonesbury Act.*

• *The novel* 1984 *written by George Orwell, is a* **satirical** **(adjectival form)** *political account of an ever-observing state that controls its citizens through fear and punishment. Also, the movie "Doctor Strangelove" is a* **satirical** *film about an insane general's efforts to start a nuclear war.*

SAWBUCK
(saw buck)

Noun. A frame that is used to hold wood while it is being sawed. In the United States, the word is also slang for a ten-dollar bill.

• *"It cost me two* **sawbucks** *and a lot of time."*

SCATHING
(**ska** theeng)

> *Adj.* **Harshly critical. Scornful and sarcastic. Bitterly severe. Strongly disapproving and condemning. Severely and glaringly critical.**

> • *Prompted by a low forecast, the sales manager sent a* **scathing** *email to all of the field managers admonishing their sales performance.*

> • *After extensive study, the United States Senate Select Committee on Ethics issued a* **scathing** *report censuring the actions of the senator.*

SCRUPULOUS
(**skroo** pew lus)

> *Adj.* **The primary meaning is having scruples. A strong sense of what is right and what is wrong. Highly principled. The secondary meaning is that which is characterized by extreme care. Painstakingly precise or exact. Minutely careful.**

> • *Without question, he is an unprincipled man, totally devoid of* **scruples** (**noun form**)*, who has left the flotsam of three failed marriages in his wake.*

> • *His work is always timely and accurate because of his* **scrupulous** *attention to detail.*

> • *During a performance evaluation, the manager must be* **scrupulously** (**adverbial form**) *attentive to what he or she says to the employee. If it is stated that a 5% to 10% raise will be recommended for approval, the only thing the employee heard is a 10% raise is forthcoming!*

SECEDE
(suh **seed**)

>*Verb.* **To withdraw or break away from an association, alliance or federation. To become independent or to disaffiliate.**

> • *Because of certain political disagreements, a few member nations **seceded** from the federation.*

> • *The act of seceding is called **secession** (noun form). We are familiar with this term in American history since it refers to the attempted withdrawal of eleven Southern states from the Union in 1860 that led to the Civil War.*

SECULAR
(**sek** u lur)

>*Adj.* **Concerned with or pertaining to the affairs of this world. Not religious or spiritual. Dealing with temporal or worldly subjects. Not ecclesiastical or clerical.**

> • *He held strong **secular** notions on the separation of church and state even though he was both a political activist and a minister of a recognized faith*

> • *The repertoire of this particular vocal group contains both religious and **secular** music.*

SEDULOUS
(**sej** u lous)

>*Adj.* **Diligent and consistent in application. Deliberately continued. Persevering. Persistent. Unwearied. Continually industrious.**

• *While it took considerable time, we successfully completed our objectives because of the **sedulous** efforts of everyone in this room.*

• *The FBI agents were in **sedulous** pursuit of the kidnappers.*

• *There are a few members on the Board of Directors who have **sedulously** (**adverbial form**) pressed for a newer and more updated national advertising campaign.*

SELF-EVIDENT
(**self-ev** uh dent)

Adj. **Evident in and of itself. Obvious, without the need for proof. That which needs no further explanation. Axiomatic. Unmistakable.**

• *When Thomas Jefferson drafted the Declaration of Independence, he held certain truths to be **self-evident**. He wrote that all men were created equal, endowed with certain unalienable rights, and among them were life, liberty and the pursuit of happiness.*

• *The mistakes are glaring and **self-evident**.*

SEMPER FIDELIS
(**sem** per fee **day** lis)

(Latin) Always Faithful. It is the motto of the U. S. Marine Corps.

SENTIMENT
(**sen** tuh ment)

Noun. **A mental feeling. An opinion or judgment caused by some feeling. The emotion felt after reading or hearing some expression as compared to exactly what is being written or said. An emotional attitude.**

• *She eloquently voiced her* **sentiments** *concerning the need to provide immediate assistance to the homeless.*

• *From coast to coast, patriotic* **sentiment** *surged after the attack on the World Trade Center.*

• *It is an inexpensive necklace that she received from her grandmother, but it has great* **sentimental** (**adjectival form**) *value to her.*

• *Concern for the poor, sick, or downtrodden is not tawdry* **sentimentalism**—*it is charity in full regalia.*

SESQUIPEDALIAN
(**ses** kwi puh **day** lee un)

Noun/Adj. **As a noun it means a long word. A word with many syllables. As an adjective it means given to using long words.**

The word is formed by combining the word element "sesqui," which means one and one half, with the word element "ped," which means foot. Thus, one and one half feet representing something extra long.

• *The wise, old professor advised the class to avoid the use of this word and the legions of words marching behind the **sesquipedalian** banner. Most **sesquipedalian** words are $25 words that should be used only if no other word expresses the idea you are attempting to convey. If clarity in your writing is the objective, then why use a word that more likely than not, will serve only to confuse and befuddle the reader. Shaking his head in mild disgust, he added that those who use sesquipedalian words are called **sesquipedalianists**—an even longer word!*

AUTHOR'S NOTE

As identified above, the word element "sesqui" means one and a half. You oftentimes see this prefix attached to the word "centennial." This means that a state celebrating its sesquicentennial is marking the completion of 150 years of statehood.

SERENDIPITOUS
(**ser** en **dip** uh tus)

Adj. **It means having the ability to make desirable but unexpected discoveries by accident. Unanticipated good fortune. An unforeseen or chance discovery of value that happens unintentionally.**

• *In the history of science, there have been many **serendipitous** discoveries that have occurred when someone accidentally discovered one thing while conducting experiments on another.*

> **Author's note**
> "Serendipitous" is a word derived from a story written by H. Walpole called *The Three Princes Of Serendip*, who had this remarkable ability. Serendip is the Arabic name for Sri Lanka, formerly Ceylon.

SHAM
(sham)

Noun. **A pretense. A hoax. An imitation purporting to be genuine but is not. Something spurious or fake. Bogus or counterfeit.**

• *It was a clever **sham** that targeted elderly couples as its victims.*

• *It is ostensibly a charitable organization providing welfare benefits to the poor. However, they cannot account for how the money is being spent or even how much has been received in donations. They appear to be a total **sham**.*

SHEEPISH
(**she** pish)

Adj. **Sheep-like. Timid. Shy. Non-assertive. Awkwardly embarrassed. Hesitant or bashful.**

• *His **sheepish** reply let everyone know he was not familiar with the subject matter.*

• *As soon as he realized he had forgotten her birthday, a **sheepish** smile crept across his face.*

SHIFTLESS
(**shift** lis)

> *Adj.* **Characterized by lack of ambition. Not resourceful. Inefficient. Lacking in incentive. Lazy. Unable to cope with certain situations. Incompetent.**

> • *He was an indolent,* **shiftless** *individual that the U. S. Army had mistakenly assigned to one of its intelligence units.*

> • *Even though it was a final examination, he was sluggish and uninspired and as a result he studied in a* **shiftless** *manner.*

SHYLOCK
(**shy** lok)

> **The relentless and shrewd moneylender in Shakespeare's** *Merchant of Venice.* **He loans money to an individual and then demands a pound of the borrower's flesh should the loan not be repaid on a timely basis.**

SIC
(**sick**)

> *Adv./Verb* **(Latin) As an adverb it is usually expressed in brackets [sic] or parentheses (sic) to indicate that something has been copied exactly from its original form even if the passage includes misspelled words, mistakes, errors, etc.**

> • *The political advisor wrote he might could* [**sic**] *persuade the President to change his position.*

As a verb it also means to incite to attack.

• She **sicced** *the dog on the would-be robber.*

SIERRA NEVADA
A mountain range in eastern California. Its highest peak is Mount Whitney (14,495 feet) near the edge of the Sequoia National Park.

SIMPLISTIC
(sim **plis** tik)

Adj. **Not complicated or elaborate. Free from complexity. Unsophisticated. Too basic. Oversimplified.**

• *To tell someone that "Success will come if you work hard," is too* **simplistic***. There are many variables that determine success.*

• *He informed us that his* **simplistic** *approach to selling was the reason he achieved his assigned goals each year. He said it was basic problem-solution selling. "Ask enough questions until you find a problem, then sell 'em the solution."*

SINE QUA NON
(**siney** kwa **non**)

(Latin) Literally translated, it means "without which not," or "without which nothing." It means something essential, vital or indispensable. Something crucial to the condition. Something within a structure that is central to maintaining relevancy and importance. Without it, the circumstances or conditions cease to exist.

• *My wife considers me her **sine qua non**.*

AUTHOR'S NOTE
This example should trigger an interesting response.

SINUOUS
(**sin** u us)

Adj. The primary meaning is having many curves. Of serpentine form. Tortuous. Winding in and out. Not straight. Moving indirectly. Twisting.

• *We followed a path next to a **sinuous** stream that forged its way down the mountain, making numerous turns and bends before finally emptying into the lake below.*

The secondary meaning is that which is characterized by agile movements. Supple and lithe.

• *There is nothing performed on stage more poetic than the **sinuous** movements of an accomplished ballet dancer.*

By extension, the third meaning of the word is devious. Not straightforward. Sneaky or underhanded. Conniving or deceitful. Not honest.

• *It appears that his desire to speak to her privately was a **sinuous** attempt to gain additional information.*

SKEPTICAL
(**skep** tuh kul)

Adj. **Doubtful. Unsure. Tending toward disbelieving. Dubious. Unconvinced or not totally persuaded.**

• *Even after lengthy explanations and assurances, the CEO remained **skeptical** over the efficacy of the plan.*

• *She was **skeptical** of his intentions.*

• *The real estate developer's report, which attempted to allay fears of traffic congestion around the proposed shopping center, was met with a great deal of **skepticism** (**noun form**) by the neighborhood association.*

✪   The opposite of "skeptical" is "convinced."

SOBRIQUET
(**so** brah **kay**)

(French) A nickname. Usually a shortened version of a longer name like Joe is for Joseph. But sobriquets can take on other forms like Jack for John and Ted for Edward or Curly for a bald-headed man.

SOLICITOUS
(suh **liss** uh tus)

Adj. **Anxious. Apprehensive. Very concerned about something. Overly attentive. Caring.**

• *Most parents are **solicitous** about their children; they want a better life for them than they had for themselves.*

• *She made **solicitous** inquiries concerning the health of his mother.*

SOLILOQUY
(suh **lil** uh kwi)

> *Noun.* **A discourse or dialog uttered by someone talking to himself. The act of talking to yourself. Also, it is used effectively in dramatic theater where the actor expresses his thoughts or feelings out loud whether he is on stage alone or with others.**

> • *One the best known **soliloquies** of all time comes from Shakespeare's* Hamlet, *the first line of which is, "To be, or not to be—that is the question."*

> • *Because he had lived alone and without companionship for so long, nightly **soliloquies** became a part of his routine.*

SORDID
(**sore** did)

> *Adj.* **Squalid. Foul and disgusting. Seedy. Dirty. Morally ignoble or degraded. Filthy.**

> • *The mayor announced plans to begin the redevelopment of a **sordid** section of the downtown business district.*

> • *No one wanted to hear the **sordid** details of his ill-gotten gains.*

SPECIOUS

(**spee** shus)

Adj. Apparently right or correct but actually false. Plausible. Seemingly truthful but actually false. Appears feasible but is not. False. Phony.

• *If we did not know all of the facts, his **specious** arguments would have been convincing.*

• *He made numerous **specious** allegations in an attempt to gain an advantage over his political opponent.*

SPLIT INFINITIVE

A split infinitive is a simple infinitive verb form with the addition of a word (usually an adverb) between the "to" and the verb. For example, "to clearly see," or "to urgently request," or "to bitterly oppose." Early usage experts condemned the use of the split infinitive. Today, however, it is a perfectly acceptable structure with many well-known authors employing its use. If you dislike the structure of the split infinitive, it is usually very easy to place the adverb elsewhere in the sentence. However, when you relocate the adverb just to avoid the split infinitive, caution should be used so that the reader is not confused. Consider the following:

• *It is difficult for me to really like classical music.*

Relocating the adverb could produce:

• *It is difficult for me to like really classical music.*

This structure makes it implicit that varying degrees of classical music exist.

The only hard and fast rule to remember regarding split infinitives is to avoid the use of multiple words between the "to" and the verb, e.g., "Our plan is to cautiously, progressively and systematically dismantle the company."

SPOONERISM
(**spoo** nuh **riz** em)

Noun. **A slip of the tongue. An error in speech. Occurs when the initial sounds of two words are accidentally transposed with humorous effect. A transposition of the initial consonant sound of one word with another.**

• *This pie is occupewed; this pew is occupied.*

• *Is the bean dizzy? Is the dean busy?*

• *You hissed my mystery lecture; you missed my history lecture.*

• *My zips are lipped; my lips are zipped.*

AUTHOR'S NOTE
The term spoonerism comes from William A Spooner (1844–1930), an English clergyman and educator who from the pulpit or the front of a lecture hall, was well known for such slip-ups.

SPURIOUS
(**spur** e us)

> *Adj.* **Bogus. False or fake. Counterfeit. Lacking authenticity. Not from a true source.**

> • *After careful examination, the curator deemed the painting to be a spurious re-creation by someone intent on defrauding an innocent collector.*

> • *Some of the statements made concerning the financial health of the company are questionable at best while others are patently spurious.*

✪   The opposite of "spurious" is "genuine."

SQUELCH
(**skwelch**)

> *Verb.* **To silence or suppress. To quell. To smother or crush. To squash. To quickly end something.**

> • *I advise each of you to quickly squelch any sign of dissension within your group.*

> • *Her attempts to squelch the rumor concerning the Vice President's health proved feckless.*

STEADFAST
(**sted fast**)

> *Adj.* **Firm and staunch. Dedicated. Resolute. Unwavering and unfaltering. Continuous commitment.**

> • *With financial and military assistance provided over*

*time, the United States has proven to be a **steadfast** ally of Israel.*

• *I would suggest that during this period of economic downturn we not waver from the **steadfast** guidelines that made our company successful.*

STOICAL
(**stow** uh kul)

> *Adj.* **Uncomplaining. Tolerant and patient. Seemingly indifferent to pain, suffering, happiness, etc. Unemotional. Passive.**

> • *The old man remained **stoical** even in the face of immense adversity.*

> • *When something bad happens to her, she will usually scream and yell and bounce off the walls. He remains so calm and unemotional. The most you might get from him is a **stoical**, "Well, that's disappointing."*

AUTHOR'S NOTE

The word "stoical" comes from a school of philosophy founded in Greece around 300 B.C. It is called Stoicism and it teaches that an individual's primary goal in life is to tend to the welfare of others. It instructs its followers to be attentive to the well being of others and by so doing will become more enlightened. This in turn will allow them to deal effectively with their own passions and emotions, thereby finding inner peace and tranquility.

STRADIVARIUS

A violin or other instrument made by an Italian named Antonio Stradivari or his family. Stradivari was born in 1644 and began making stringed instruments in Cremona, Italy. He produced violins, violas, harps and cellos. His design for the violin, however, became the standard for all violinmakers because of the richness and clarity of its tone and the volume of its sound. As a result, many counterfeit models have been made and sold at significant prices. A genuine Stradivarius is valued at two to three million dollars. Both genuine and fake violins carry a Latin inscription, *"Antonius Stradivarius Cremonensis Faciebat Anno."* Translated, it describes the maker, the city and the date. It is from this Latin label that the name Stradivarius became known. It is estimated that Stradivari produced approximately 1100 stringed instruments in his lifetime of which 600 to 650 still exist today. The best estimate is that 512 of these are the famous violin.

STRATEGIC
(stra **tee** jik)

Adj. Pertaining to the nature of strategy. Mostly a military term referring to such things as "strategic bombing missions," or "strategic targets." However, the word has passed into the business world as a reference to a corporation's overall plan to enter and maintain a presence in the marketplace. The overall plan for a corporation to market its products is called corporate strategy and is developed by analyzing the market, determining product fit and developing a plan to create market awareness.

• *Many large corporations have **strategic** planning staffs that help create the course and direction of the company.*

• *One of the objectives of our corporate **strategy** (noun form) is to market our products through third-party vendors who would purchase our products at a discount and then resell them at slightly higher margins.*

A distinction should be made between that which is strategic and that which is tactical. The overall plan is the strategic part, and the tactical part is the process by which the strategy is executed.

• *In the preceding example, the **strategic** part is the desire to market through third-party resellers or business partners. The tactical part would be hiring and training partner account managers to sell to these selected business partners.*

STRAW VOTE

An unofficial vote or polling process undertaken to determine the trend of opinion on an individual seeking public office. It is also used to describe an unofficial polling on such issues as bond elections, tax increases, etc.

STRINGENT
(**stren** jent)

Adj. **Strict. Rigorous or demanding. Precise. Rigid. Exacting. Severe.**

• *Because of the latest accident at the plant, the management of the company established more **stringent** safety measures to protect its employees.*

• *With enrollments down for the year, the Board of Regents called for tighter controls and a more **stringent** operating budget.*

✪   The opposite of "stringent" is "loose," or "flexible."

SUB-LEASE
(**sub-leese**)

Noun/Verb. **As a noun, it refers to a written document whereby a lessee of real property agrees to lease the property to another lessee, formally referred to as the sub-lessee. As a verb, it refers to the act of sub-leasing or sub-letting the property.**

• *We were able to cut operating costs by **sub-leasing** half of our existing space.*

SUBSTANTIATE
(sub **stan** she ate)

Verb. **To validate. To authenticate. To confirm or support. To provide evidence. To prove.**

• *His arguments do not **substantiate** the claims he has made.*

• *Her testimony* **substantiated** *his alibi.*

The second definition of this word means to give substance to or to make something a reality. To make something concrete or actual. To put into play.

• *I would advise each of you to take the ideas we have discussed at this meeting and* **substantiate** *them into action plans.*

The adjective "substantial" (sub **stan** shul) **on the other hand means being of considerable size, amount or degree as in a "substantial amount of money."**

SUCCINCT
(suc **singkt**)

Adj. **Concise. To the point. Brief, but clearly understood. Terse or laconic. Expressed in a few words.**

• *The wise, old professor advised his students to keep their writing clear, concise,* **succinct** *and to the point. He wanted them to avoid what he called the use of "worbage" in their writing. This was his expression built from a contraction of "words" and "garbage." The following are a few of his offerings that could be used to replace "the excessive worbage that bloats and expands our paragraphs."*

• *Owing to the fact that . . . Since*

• *In spite of the fact that . . . Although*

• *She did not pay any attention to . . . She ignored*

• *There is no doubt but that . . . Doubtless*

• *Call your attention to the fact . . . Remind you*

• *The question as to whether . . . Whether*

• *The reason why is that . . . Because*

• *It is interesting to note that . . . Interestingly*

• *It is important to realize that . . . Recognize*

• *He reminded them on numerous occasions that clear and* **succinctly** (adverbial form) *written paragraphs take time and effort. It is all too easy to include the trite and hackneyed phrases that are so prevalent today. But, concise writing demands their removal from any communication. He recounted the story of one of his students who a few months after graduation sent an email to bring him up to date on what was happening in her life. Looking at the long-winded email, the professor thought she had forgotten one of the principal rules of concise writing until he read the last line of her missive. "Professor, I am sorry this email is so long, but I didn't have time to write you a shorter one."*

Remember the words of the wise, old professor: "Concise writing takes time and effort."

SUFFIX
(**suff** iks)

> *Verb/Noun.* **As a verb the word means to add or annex at the end of something. To append. To join or add on. The word is more commonly used in grammar, however, as a noun to indicate a word element, letter or group of letters added at the end of a word to make a new word.**

> • *By adding the **suffix** "ly" to the adjective "quick," the word is transformed into the adverb "quickly."*

> • *Some common **suffixes** include:*

> *–ment to form entertain**ment**.*

> *–ship to form friend**ship**.*

> *–less to form home**less**.*

> *–able to form knowledge**able**.*

> *–ful to form plenti**ful**.*

AUTHOR'S NOTE
There is obvious confusion by some over the spelling of the suffix "ful" when they attempt to use two "l's" for the suffix (full). You can avoid this uncertainty by knowing that all forms of this suffix, such as "beautiful," "hopeful," "thankful," or "useful," have only one "l."

SUFFRAGE
(**suff** rij)

Noun. **The right to vote in an election. The exercise of such a right.**

• *It is difficult to believe that it took so long for the women's* **suffrage** *movement to finally achieve results. Heroic women such as Elizabeth Stanton (1815 – 1902) and Susan B. Anthony (1820 – 1906), various social welfare groups and reform-minded politicians worked tirelessly to grant women the right to vote. It was not until 1920—**just one long lifetime ago**—that women were given voting status with the passage of the 19th Amendment to the Constitution.*

SULLY
(**sull** e)

Verb. **A versatile word that is used frequently both literally and figuratively. Literally, it means to tarnish. To soil. To taint or discolor.**

• *Because of the careless manner in which it had been stored, the silverware became* **sullied** *over time.*

It is also used figuratively to denote an action that dishonors, smears, discredits or defiles.

• *The company she kept* **sullied** *her reputation.*

✪ The opposite of "sully" is "praise" or "exalt."

SUMMARILY
(suh **mare** uh lee)

> *Adv.* **This word is the adverbial form of the word "summary." A summary is a brief or concise rendering of a larger body of material. An abridgement or an abstract. The result of something reduced to its main points usually in an effort to save time. Thus, summarily means promptly. Without delay. Without attention to formalities. Unceremoniously fast. In a summary manner. Quickly. Hastily.**

> • *Since this is the third year in a row that he has failed to achieve his sales objectives, he should be **summarily** relieved of his responsibilities.*

> • *Once he heard all the facts, the judge deemed the lawsuit to be frivolous and **summarily** dismissed the case.*

SUPERCILIOUS
(**sue** purr **sil** e us)

> *Adj.* **Having or showing arrogant superiority. Disdainful. Haughty and self-important. Pompous and condescending. Snooty. Snobbish.**

> • *Rest assured you will get a **supercilious** comment from her if you inadvertently breach the rules of etiquette.*

> • *Though he was brilliant at devising strategic military maneuvers, most of those in the general's command despised his **supercilious** demeanor.*

SUPERFLUOUS
(sue **purr** flu us)

> *Adj.* **Surplus. Extra. Unnecessary. Exorbitant or excessive. Something made unnecessary by superabundance. Non-essential.**

> • *The wise, old professor advised those in the class to cautiously edit everything they write and delete all* ***superfluous*** *words.*

> • *His parents had spent endless hours advising him on the trials and tribulations of college life, and now here was his uncle offering more* ***superfluous*** *advice.*

✪ The opposite of "superfluous" is "essential," "vital," or "crucial."

AUTHOR'S NOTE
The following is an excellent example of removing unneeded or unnecessary words when constructing sentences. The first attempt at drafting an example for the word "refurbish" in this text is presented below. Upon rewrite, the five italicized words were removed and one new word was added.

First Draft

[They were simply old ideas and principles *that were* refurbished with *the* new information *that resulted* from current testing and experimentation.]

Upon Rewrite
[They were simply old ideas and principles refurbished with new information gained from current testing and experimentation.]

(17 WORDS VS. 21 WORDS—
A 19% REDUCTION)

SUPERLATIVE
(suh **purr** luh tive)

>*Adj./Noun.* **As an adjective it means unmatched or unparalleled. Exceptional. Surpassing all others. Beyond compare. Incomparable. Sterling.**
>
>• *Lance Armstrong turned in a **superlative** performance in capturing his seventh consecutive Tour de France title.*
>
>**As a noun it is a grammatical term expressing the degree of comparison that is unsurpassed.**
>
>• *Good—better—best. "Best" is the **superlative** of "good."*
>
>**It also means an exaggerated expression. Something inflated or enlarged to an abnormal degree.**
>
>• *The critics lavished copious **superlatives** on his performance.*

SUPPLANT
(suh **plant**)
> *Verb.* **To replace. To unseat. To take the place of. To displace through strategy or intrigue.**

> • *A much younger man, who captured the imagination of the local voters with his charm and wit, **supplanted** the mayor.*

> • *The typewriter has been part of the business world for decades. Today, however, the computer has **supplanted** the typewriter.*

SUPPOSITION
(sup uh **zish** en)
> *Noun.* **The act of supposing. Something that is assumed. Considered as a possibility. An assumption. A hypothesis. A belief without supporting evidence.**

> • *That particular theory is based on the **supposition** that life exists on other planets.*

> • *There have been conflicting studies over the **supposition** that students from wealthier and more affluent families achieve higher academic marks than students from lower income families.*

SURMISE
(sur **mize**)
> *Verb.* **To guess. To logically deduce. To assume or to presume. To suppose. To infer from scanty evidence.**

• *Since I do not see your baggage, I **surmise** you will not be joining us on the trip.*

• *The FBI investigators **surmised** that the extortionists had fled the country.*

SURREPTITIOUS
(**sur** up **tish** us)

> *Adj.* **Sneaky. Covert or secretive. Clandestine. Underhanded or undercover. An action not known to the general public. Furtive.**
>
> • *In the dark of night, the burglars made a **surreptitious** entry into the bank building.*
>
> • *While no one doubted he had accumulated great wealth, many felt his success was achieved by **surreptitious** methods.*

✪ The opposite of "surreptitious" is "honest" or "open."

SVENGALI
(sven **gaul** e)

> **Svengali is the name of an evil character from a novel entitled *Trilby*, written by George Du Maurier (1834–1896). Svengali was an unsuccessful musician who enticed a young female singer, Trilby, to submit to his hypnotic suggestions. He thereby transformed her into a brilliant concert performer and lived in luxury as a result of her fame. She always performed in a hypnotic state and was oblivious to her split personality. Today,**

the term Svengali is used to refer to anyone who
exercises a controlling or powerful influence over
another.

SYBARITE
(**sib** uh rite)

> *Noun.* **A lover of luxury. One addicted to the
> pleasures of the senses. One devoted to sensual
> pleasures. A voluptuary. A sensualist. One who
> makes physical enjoyment his primary goal. One
> who seeks the gratification of sensual appetites.**

> • *He is a self-proclaimed* **sybarite** *who revels in the
> luxuries and sensual pleasures that life has to offer.*

> • *The thick oriental rugs, soft music, and the heavily
> cushioned pillows on the floor were all evidences of her*
> **sybaritic** (**adjectival form**) *lifestyle.*

SYCOPHANT
(**sik** uh funt)

> *Noun.* **A person who flatters to gain an advantage.
> A person who excessively adulates. One who
> fawns over another. One who exploits the rich
> and famous and earns acceptance by flattery. One
> who attempts to please another to gain favor.**

> • *On most days,* **sycophants** *surrounded the rich and
> powerful prince.*

> • *One could hear* **sycophantic** (**adjectival form**)
> *laughter emanating from the boardroom as once again
> the chairman made his feeble attempts at humor.*

SYMPATHETIC
(**sim** puh **thet** ik)

Adj. **The first meaning of this word is having similar tastes and inclinations. Not antagonistic. Agreeable to one's own mood or disposition.**

• *Because their views on life were so similar, he found her to be a most **sympathetic** companion.*

The second meaning entails understanding. Being compassionate. Caring and considerate. Having sensitivity to others' emotions. It means the state of being simultaneously affected with the same emotions or feelings of another.

• *She found great solace in his caring and **sympathetic** words.*

Do not confuse "sympathetic" with "empathetic." "Empathetic" is showing mental comprehension for another's feelings. Perceiving another's mental state, but not feeling the same emotion.

• *He was fortunate to have an understanding and **empathetic** school advisor to assist him.*

• *She was a brilliant photographer whose **empathetic** images documented the plight of the homeless.*

SYNERGY
(**sin** er gee)

Noun. **Also synergism. Refers to the combined effect of two or more elements to produce a** result that is greater than the individual effects. Combined action. In medicine, it refers to the healthy interaction of every organ of a particular system, e.g., the digestive system. In business, companies are merged or acquired for the expected added benefit of the union.

AUTHOR'S NOTE
The following is a portion of a sales report copied exactly as written by a branch sales manager to his vice president of sales.

• *"We formed a sales team by combining two individuals with differing personality traits, and the resulting synergy has been remarkable. Mark is outgoing, gregarious and gets along well with our customers. He is friendly and always upbeat. Harold, on the other hand, operates on a different wavelength. He is quiet and reserved, but highly gifted. He has an overwhelming understanding of our technology and how our products function, but is sorely lacking in interpersonal skills. So much so, that when you say hello to him in the morning, he is sometimes stumped for an answer."*

SYNTAX
(**sin** tax)

Syntax is that part of grammar in a particular language which deals with the structure and formation of phrases and sentences. It is the study of word order or pattern in a sentence according to established and historical usage.

SYSTEMIC
(sis **tem** ik)

Adj. The word means that which concerns or relates to a system. That which is common to a system. In physiology, it means that which affects the entire body or organism or a particular body system, especially the nervous system. In the business world, it often refers to a scheme or structure.

• *The problems we were experiencing in our accounting department were **systemic** in nature and continued to haunt us until we completely overhauled our systems and procedures.*

• *An increased crime rate, burgeoning court dockets and over crowded jails indicate the need for a **systemic** change in our jurisprudence system.*

TACIT
(**tas** it)

Adj. Silent. Not openly or directly expressed, but implied. Something that is not stated, but is understood or inferred. That which is unspoken, but deduced.

• *We knew we had his **tacit** consent when he offered no objections to our plan.*

• *Since we received no comments from her department, we assumed she **tacitly** (**adverbial form**) supported the advertising initiative we had outlined.*

✪   The opposite of "tacit" is "explicit" or "forth-right."

TACITURN
(**tas** uh **turn**)

> *Adj.* **Quiet. Habitually silent. Reticent to speak. Not forthcoming. Tight-lipped and uncommunicative. Reserved in speech.**

> • *After the interview, the manager concluded that the interviewee's **taciturn** nature would preclude him from becoming an effective sales person.*

> • *His actions were enigmatic. At times he would be secretive and **taciturn** and at other times garrulous and demonstrative.*

TALE OF TWO CITIES

> *A Tale of Two Cities* **is a classic historical novel written in 1859 by Charles Dickens. The two cities are Paris and London, and the setting is during the time of the French Revolution. The story is noteworthy for its dramatic depiction of France during this turbulent time. It has been so widely read that even today, a portion of the first line of the first chapter of the book is often quoted in various speeches and addresses: "It was the best of times, it was the worst of times. . . ."**

TALISMAN
(**tal** us mun)

> *Noun.* **A charm. An amulet. A trinket or piece of jewelry worn to bring good fortune or to**

magically increase one's power or for protection against evil.

• *She felt strongly that the **talisman** she wore every day protected her from various diseases.*

• *On his way to class to take the final examination in English, he slipped the small **talisman** into his pocket for good luck. His father had given it to him, and so far it had never failed.*

TANDEM
(**tan** dem)

Adv. **One behind the other. Not abreast. Similar to a horse drawn carriage with horses in single file or a bicycle built for two. Any group of two or more arranged one behind the other, but operating or acting in conjunction with each other.**

• *In 1996 an IBM RS6000 computer made history by defeating world champion chess player, Garry Kasparov, in a game of chess. It was the first time a computer had defeated a world champion under tournament conditions. Nicknamed "Big Blue," the machine used 256 processors operating in **tandem**. Incredibly, it could evaluate thousands of chess positions per second.*

TANGENTIAL
(tan **jen** shul)

Adj. **Similar to a tangent. Moving in the direction of a tangent. More commonly, the word is used to describe something of superficial relevance. Merely touching. Slightly connected. Incidental.**

Something that is peripheral. Not of central importance.

• Her **tangential** remarks were interesting, but not totally applicable to the problem we were trying to solve.

• While he had opened a few doors for her, he had only **tangential** involvement in her success.

✪   The opposite of "tangential" is "central."

TANTAMOUNT
(**tan** tuh **mount**)

Adj. Equivalent to. The same as. Equal in value, force, significance, etc. Practically the same. Indistinguishable. Equal in effect.

• Considering the president issued the inquiry, I feel his request is **tantamount** to a demand.

• Fraternizing with enemy troops in time of war is **tantamount** to treason.

• In his retirement address to the employees, the chairman cautioned them to avoid doing things a certain way because that is how it had always been done in the past. He challenged them to move away from the pitfalls of this logic, since to do otherwise is **tantamount** to saying there is no need for individual expression, no need for individual creativity, and no need for the entrepreneurial spirit upon which the industry was formed.

TCHAIKOVSKY, PYOTR

Tchaikovsky (1840–1893) is easily the most popular and well-known Russian composer of all time. He has received worldwide acclaim for his poignant melodies, memorable harmonies and impressive orchestrations. He is most known for his symphony, *Romeo and Juliet*, his ballets, *Swan Lake, Sleeping Beauty and The Nutcracker*, for his *Piano Concerto No. 1*, and for the *1812 Overture*.

TELL, WILLIAM

The story of William Tell is of questionable authenticity. He is said to have lived in Switzerland in the early 14th century and was an expert with a crossbow. The Austrian governor, Hermann Gessler, reportedly erected a pole in the town square with his hat perched on top. All of the townsfolk were to bow before it as they passed by. William Tell refused to do so and was arrested. He was given the choice of shooting an apple off the top of his son's head or dying. He chose the former and successfully completed the daring feat. When asked why he brought two arrows to the event, he informed Gessler that had he killed his son he would have used the second arrow on him. Gessler became enraged and attempted to arrest Tell a second time. Tell escaped only to return later and kill Gessler. To the townsfolk, Tell was hailed as a hero. This one act of defiance sparked a rebellion that later led to Switzerland's independence. The German poet and dramatist, Friedrich Schiller, later wrote a play called *Wilhelm Tell*, which in turn inspired operatic composer, Gioacchino Rossini, to compose in 1829 the *William Tell Overture*. A portion of that overture that Rossini intended to represent the galloping horses of the Swiss Army was later adopted as the theme song for *The Lone Ranger*.

TEMERITY
(tuh **mare** uh tee)

Noun. **Recklessness. Foolhardy disregard of danger. Unreasonable lack of fear. Gall. Flagrant boldness. Nerve. Audacity.**

• *Diving into the waters below without knowing the depth was a foolish display of* **temerity**.

• *Although we don't know the full extent of the personal reasons she cited, we admire her* **temerity** *in turning down the promotion.*

Do not confuse "temerity" with the word "timorous" (tim er us), which has almost the opposite meaning. "Timorous" is an adjective that means nervous or fearful. Lacking in courage. Afraid. Timid. Apprehensive.

• *He had* **timorous** *doubts about his ability to give an effective presentation to such a large audience.*

TEMPESTUOUS
(tim **pes** choo us)

Adj. **Relating to or characterized by tempests. A tempest is a violent current of wind, especially one accompanied by rain, hail or snow. A violent storm. More commonly the word is used to denote** that which is stormy, turbulent or intense. That which is uncontrolled and passionate. Raging or wild.

• *The two political leaders engaged in a **tempestuous** debate as each tried to prove the validity of their positions on the major issues of the campaign.*

• *Their **tempestuous** relationship was finally ended when they agreed that divorce was the only answer.*

TERTIARY
(**tur** she air e)

Noun/Adj. **As a noun it identifies a carbon atom united to three other atoms. Geologically, it pertains to a geological period from 2 million to 63 million years ago. More commonly, the word is used to denote something in the third rank or order. Third in terms of importance or value. Subsequent to that which is secondary. Third.**

• *The board of directors agreed that the new executive compensation plan provides incentives that would both motivate and retain top-level executives within the firm. They also believe the plan provides a **tertiary** benefit by making it easier to attract other talented executives from within the industry.*

TORPID
TURBID
TURGID

Author's note

These three words have been grouped together because they look and sound so much alike. It probably explains why they have seen such limited action in our verbal and written communications. Placing them together will assist you in understanding their differences. A mnemonic—memory assisting—device is provided that will allow you to always remember the definition of each word. As you go through each word, key on the letter in parenthesis and the word associated with it.

TORPID Tor(p)id p-passive
(**tor** pid)

Adj. **Passive. Sluggish. Lazy or lethargic. Inactive. Languid.**

• *While his advisors pressed for a more active and vigorous campaign, the politically **torpid** mayor proceeded at his own pace.*

• *He could accept the loss of physical strength and ability, but found it more arduous to abide the sense of inevitability of a mind grown **torpid** with the passing years.*

✪   The opposite of "torpid" is "active" or "energetic."

TURBID Tur(b)id b-blurry
(**tur** bid)

> *Adj.* **Blurry. Opaque. Murky or unclear as sediment in wine. Dense. Cloudy. Lack of clarity or direction.**

> • *A **turbid** creek wound itself through the property.*

> • *His life had come crashing down, and suddenly he found himself immersed in the **turbid** depths of misery and loneliness.*

✪   The opposite of "turbid" is "clear."

TURGID Tur(g)id g-gaseous
(**tur** jid)

> *Adj.* **Swollen or inflated as with gas. Enlarged beyond what is normal. Metaphorically, the word is used to describe someone who is vainly ostentatious. Showy. Pompous. Full of self-importance. Pretentious or grandiose. Idiomatically, "full of hot air." Bloated.**

> • *The baseball accident left the side of his face bruised and **turgid**.*

> • *The Southern senator had gained a reputation as a political figure given to bombastic and **turgid** oratories.*

✪ The opposite of "turgid" is "understated," or "down-to-earth."

TORTUOUS
(**tor** chur us)

> *Adj.* **That which is twisting or winding. Meandering. Full of twists and turns. Crooked or roundabout. Circuitous.**

• *It was difficult to steer the truck down the **tortuous** road.*

The word is also used to describe that which is not direct in procedure, method or policy. Not conclusively direct, as in "tortuous logic" or "tortuous reasoning."

Do not confuse "tortuous" with "torturous" (tor chur us)**, which is the adjectival form of the word "torture," meaning to inflict pain. Causing intense mental or physical pain. Abusive treatment to gain information.**

AUTHOR'S NOTE
The word calls to mind the non-tortuous conclusion reached by the late Bishop Fulton J. Sheen when discussing criminal activity. He said, "A river always follows the line of least resistance. That's why it's crooked."

TRACTABLE
(**trak** tuh bul)

Adj. **Easily managed. Easily controlled. Obedient and well-mannered. Docile. Compliant. Cooperative or amenable. Malleable.**

• *The new chief information officer quickly realized that one of his major obstacles would be directing an aging group of departmental employees that seemed to be neither cooperative nor **tractable**.*

• *One of the great joys of teaching is the opportunity to witness first hand those students who have **tractable** young minds coupled with an intense desire to learn.*

TRANQUIL
(**trang** kwil)

Adj. **Calm. Serene. Peaceful. Free from commotion. Free from turmoil. Quiet and restful. Unruffled. Sedate.**

• *He wanted to escape the burdens of the work-a-day world, so he bought a small house in the mountains bordering a **tranquil** blue lake.*

• *To his lament, the peace and **tranquility** (**noun form**) he had hoped to enjoy in retirement were constantly interrupted by financial constraints.*

✪   The opposite of "tranquil" is "loud," or "noisy."

TRANSGRESS
(tranz **gress**)

Verb. **To overstep. To go over the limit. To go beyond the boundaries. To break, e.g., the law. To run afoul of that which is customary or standard.**

• *His lewd and licentious behavior* **transgressed** *the bounds of propriety.*

• *The Major explained his "Rules of the Road" to the new recruits and informed them that anyone* **transgressing** *these rules would be dealt with summarily.*

The word "transcend" (tran send) is a verb with a somewhat similar meaning. However, "transcend" is different from "transgress" in that it implies going over, exceeding or excelling some limit in a positive manner. It does not carry the negative connotation of "transgress." It means to surpass, to overshadow or rise above.

• *Her performance* **transcended** *the expectations of even her most loyal advocates.*

TRANSITORY
(**tran** suh **tor** e)

Adj. **Brief. Fleeting. Lasting a short time. Not permanent or enduring. Of short duration. Not persistent. Temporary.**

• *As one ages, there is an overwhelming propensity to reflect on the* **transitory** *nature of youth.*

• *Some forms of depression are* **transitory***, while others require long-term medical attention.*

• *He felt that most of the problems he was experiencing at the office were* **transitory** *and would soon pass.*

TRAVESTY
(**trav** us tee)

> *Noun.* **The treatment of a respected and noble subject in a trivial manner. An exaggerated or mocking imitation. A farce. Idiomatically, "a take-off on." A shameless imitation. A serious matter treated frivolously. An imitation. A mockery of a serious subject.**

> • *There are many who consider the murder trial of O. J. Simpson to be a* **travesty** *of justice.*

TRUCULENT
(**truk** u lent)

> *Adj.* **Disposed to fight. Hostile. Quarrelsome. Defiant and argumentative. Combative. Pugnacious. Cruel and bullying.**

> • *She took an unpopular position on the issue, so she should not be surprised at the* **truculent** *criticism she has received.*

> • *A large crowd gathered outside of city hall to* **truculently** **(adverbial form)** *assert their opposition to what they believe is a violation of their civil rights.*

> ✪ The opposite of "truculent" is "amiable," "friendly," or "good-natured."

TRUNCATE
(**trung** kate)
>*Verb.* **To cut short. To abbreviate. To decrease in length. To trim or pare. To curtail or shorten. Abruptly terminate.**
>
>• *The producer felt it necessary to **truncate** the television movie in order to air a late breaking news story.*
>
>• *His speech was **truncated** by jeers from the audience.*

✪   The opposite of "truncate" is "lengthen," or "increase."

TURBULENT
(**tur** bu lent)
>*Adj.* **Unstable. Having a chaotic or restless characteristic. Agitated. Unruly. Raging or riotous. Disorderly. Disturbed. Characterized by unrest.**
>
>• *With rain continuing, the **turbulent** rapids seemed to be gaining in force and intensity.*
>
>• *It is problematic that the sixties would have been so **turbulent** had President John Kennedy not been assassinated.*

UBIQUITOUS
(u **bik** wuh tus)
>*Adj.* **Being everywhere or seeming to be everywhere at the same time. Present everywhere. Omnipresent. Universal. All-pervading. Encountered or found everywhere.**

• *The great spoiler of the Sunday afternoon picnic is the* **ubiquitous** *little ant.*

• *One of the dreadful tragedies of our society is the* **ubiquitous** *use of mind-altering drugs*

• *Over the past several years, the retailing landscape has been changed significantly by the* **ubiquitous** *fast food outlets found on every street corner.*

✪   The opposite of "ubiquitous" is "rare."

UNABASHED
(**un** uh **bashed**)

Adj. **Unembarrassed. Unashamed. Not disguised. Open and blatant. Without apology.**

• *The waiter's* **unabashed** *fawning over her made it clear that not many celebrities visited this restaurant.*

• *It was amazing that he remained so* **unabashed** *after making such an egregious social error.*

• *He loudly and* **unabashedly** (adverbial form) *voiced his disgust when our reports failed to reach him in a timely manner.*

UNABATED
(**un** uh **bay** tid)

Adj. **Undiminished. Continuing in full force. No reduction in intensity. Not subdued. Idiomatically, "in full swing." Maintaining full force. Sustained.**

• *Although she passed away several years ago, the popularity of her music has been **unabated**.*

• *Notwithstanding the criticisms of the literati, he fought with **unabated** intensity for the acceptance of his philosophical theories.*

UNABRIDGED
(**un** uh **brijd**)

Adj. **Not abridged. Not shortened. Not condensed. Comprehensive. Whole. Un-cut. Full-length. Complete.**

• *We received an **unabridged** copy of the novel.*

• *An **unabridged** dictionary is one not reduced in size by the elimination of words or definitions. It is a comprehensive edition.*

UNANIMITY
(**u** nuh **nim** uh tee)

Noun. **Complete agreement. Everyone being of one mind. Total accord. The state of being unanimous. A confluence of minds. One accord, one voice.**

• *All of the financial advisors were in **unanimity** on their recommendation to the management committee to delay the IPO until market conditions were more favorable.*

• *Our technologists are in complete **unanimity** on the need to install new database technology.*

AUTHOR'S NOTE

Generally, a majority of votes by a group empowers the group to act as a whole, e.g., the legislature can pass a law when a majority is in favor of the issue. On the other hand, a jury can only decide an issue or decide someone's fate if the vote is unanimous.

UNASSAILABLE
(**un** uh **sail** uh bul)

Adj. **Not attackable. Impregnable. Unquestionable. Sound or watertight. Iron clad or not open to doubt as in "unassailable logic" or "unassailable truths." Impossible to dispute or disprove. Irrefutable. Impenetrable. Secure. Able to withstand an assault.**

• *In an effort to protect the city's inhabitants, they built an **unassailable** fortress at the mouth of the river.*

• *To safeguard their computer environments from digital attacks, many companies have gone beyond simple detection procedures and have installed complex system devices that make their computer systems virtually **unassailable**.*

✪   The opposite of "unassailable" is "vulnerable."

UNCONSCIONABLE
(un **kon** shun uh bul)

Adj. Having no conscience. Exceeding the bounds of what is just or reasonable. Unscrupulous. Unreasonable. Obscene. Preposterous. Grossly exceeding that which is normal. Beyond that which is prudent. Unprincipled.

• *It is easy to understand those critics who chastised this administration for what they felt was an* **unconscionable** *act in allocating funds to study the effects of the tsetse fly on the rain forests and to study the effects of the un-cushioned toilet seat on the sacroiliac.*

Author's note
Taken from an actual letter written to a wireless telephone company by a disgruntled user whose phone frequently failed to work each time he traveled out of the city

---

• *".... the answers to those questions raised in my previous letter are essential to arriving at a final resolution to our dispute. To decide to not answer them is surely the apex of negligent business practices and is simply* **unconscionable.** *"*

UNDAUNTED
(un **don** tid)

Adj. Fearless. Courageous. Firm of purpose. Resolutely brave. Intrepid. Bold. Not disturbed or discouraged. Not shackled by fear. Bravery in the face of danger.

• *The **undaunted** marine entered the village and single-handedly rescued the remaining civilians.*

• *We all knew his illness was terminal. But we had great admiration for this man, who with an **undaunted** spirit housed in a tragically frail body, was waging the fight of his life.*

✪ The opposite of "undaunted" is "fearful."

UNDERPIN
(**un** dur **pin**)

> *Verb.* **To support from underneath. To provide a foundation as with masonry or props. To bolster or to buttress. It is also used to mean support for ideas, notions, movements or policies. To validate. To confirm. To support with evidence. To corroborate.**

• *The economists concluded that increased export activity **underpins** the country's phenomenal growth.*

• *In order to enhance her position, she provided numerous references that **underpinned** her conclusions.*

✪ The opposite of "underpin" is "weaken."

UNEQUIVOCAL
(**un** e **kwiv** uh kul)

> *Adj.* **Clear or clear-cut. Obvious. Not ambiguous. Clearly defined. Definite and distinct. Without qualification or exception. Straightforward and apparent.**

• *Students in law school quickly learn the necessarily* **unequivocal** *nature of the language of laws.*

• *Research studies conclude* **unequivocally** (**adverbial form**) *that violent computer games and television shows increase the likelihood of aggressive and violent behavior in children.*

✪   The opposite of "unequivocal" is "equivocal," or "vague."

UNFETTER
(un **fet** er)

Verb. **To release from fetters (chains or shackles). To release. To untie or unbind. To unbridle. To free from restrictions or bonds. To unchain or unshackle. To set free.**

• *He encouraged his managers to* **unfetter** *their minds from the restraints of old policies and procedures and to idiomatically, "think outside the box."*

• *As a nationally known journalist, he continually opposed governmental limitations on freedom of speech. Over time, he became the unofficial spokesman for an* **unfettered** (**adjectival form**) *press.*

✪   The opposite of "unfetter" is "hold," "bind," or "restrain."

UNFLINCHING
(un **flin** ching)

Adj. **Unwavering. Constant and unremitting.**

Fearless. Steadfast in the eyes of danger. Not intimidated. Showing no fear. Resolute. Dogged and persistent. Unrelenting.

• *He had that unique ability to face all challenges with* **unflinching** *courage.*

• *Despite declining public opinion, he remained* **unflinching** *in his defense of the government's reconstruction plan for the small Asian country.*

AUTHOR'S NOTE

One of the most descriptive quotations regarding this characteristic was issued by the late Secretary of State Dean Rusk when evaluating a conciliatory move made by the U.S.S.R. at the height of the Cuban missile crisis. "We're eyeball to eyeball, and I think the other fellow just blinked."

UNILATERAL
(**u** nuh **lat** er ul)

> *Adj.* **One-sided. Involving only one side. One party. That which is undertaken by only one person or group. Obligations or actions of only one side.**

• *It was a* **unilateral** *decision that sparked considerable opposition.*

• *The plan called for a* **unilateral** *disengagement of Israel from occupied Palestinian lands.*

"Bilateral" means having two sides. Joint. Affecting reciprocally two parties or two groups. That which is undertaken by two sides.

"Multilateral" means several or many sides, e.g., "a multilateral trade agreement" affecting several nations.

"Bipartisan" refers to two parties, e.g., a "bipartisan forum" composed of both Democrats and Republicans.

UNMITIGATED
(un **mit** uh **gay** tid)

Adj. Not qualified in any way. Not moderated in intensity. Pure or absolute. Not softened. Complete. Utter. Not diminished by any other fact or condition. Not lessened.

• *Because he had so much to gain from the decision, we all felt his account of what happened was an* **unmitigated** *lie.*

• *When you consider the time and effort that was expended, this venture is simply an* **unmitigated** *disaster.*

UNRELENTING
(**un** ree **len** ting)

Adj. Continual. Never ceasing. Persistent. Not weakening in strength or vigor. Indefatigable. Unremitting. Constant. Not diminished in desire or determination.

• *Married couples with children oftentimes feel pressured by the* **unrelenting** *demands of parenthood.*

• *With over 40 million people infected with HIV worldwide, the disease appears to be* **unrelenting** *and even outpacing medical efforts to contain it.*

UNREQUITED
(**un** ree **kwi** tid)

> *Adj.* **Unanswered. That which is not reciprocated. Not returned. Not repaid. Not given back. Not returned in the same way or degree.**

> • *After her death, they discovered an unpublished diary with numerous entries lamenting an* **unrequited** *love.*

> • *He took no retaliatory action: letting it lie as an* **unrequited** *injustice.*

UNTENABLE
(un **ten** uh bul)

> *Adj.* **Indefensible. Unjustified. Not capable of being logical. Flawed. Unsound or weak. Idiomatically, "on shaky ground." Not capable of being defended.**

> • *The posture taken by India that Kashmir is an integral part of India is, according to Pakistani leaders, an* **untenable** *position.*

> • *The notion that we can increase sales by simply adding head count is* **untenable**. *We must stay focused on profitability.*

✪ The opposite of "untenable" is "plausible," "rational," or "watertight."

UNTOWARD
(un **tord**)

> *Adj.* **The primary meaning is socially unacceptable. Not proper. Unbefitting or unseemly. Unbecoming or indecent. Not in keeping with accepted standards. Idiomatically, "out of line."**
>
> • *At the conclusion of the campus-wide party, the university police reported no* **untoward** *incidents.*
>
> **The secondary meaning is troublesome or unpleasant. Adverse. Harmful. That which is not in your best interests. Undesirable.**
>
> • *You have to admire her strength and determination in making a life for herself under* **untoward** *circumstances.*

URBANE
(er **bane**)

> *Adj.* **Suave and sophisticated. Effortlessly gracious. Polished. Smooth. Showing a high level of refinement. Cosmopolitan. Debonair. Refined and genteel. Cultured.**
>
> • *He was Harvard educated, handsome and a Boston aristocrat. Probably no other president, before or since, has exhibited the easy style and* **urbane** *qualities of John F. Kennedy.*

UTILITARIAN
(u **till** uh **tare** e en)

> *Adj.* Useful. Functional. Practical. As distinguished from that which is decorative or ornamental. Pragmatic. Serviceable. Having a useful function. Workaday. Regard for utility versus beauty.

> • *The young couple determined that at this point in their lives it would be more prudent to purchase **utilitarian** furniture pieces rather than those with more elaborate designs.*

✪　The opposite of "utilitarian" is "useless."

VACILLATE
(**vas** uh late)

> *Verb.* To waver. To move from side to side or back and forth. To fluctuate. Rising and falling in a wavelike pattern. To move one way and then another. Relative to opinions or actions, it means to be indecisive. To waffle. To waver between conflicting positions.

> • *He **vacillated** between retiring early or continuing to work.*

> • *Our campaign has been damaged because of his tendency to **vacillate** on some of the major issues.*

✪　The opposite of "vacillate" is "decide," or "choose."

VACUOUS
(**vak** u us)

> *Adj.* Empty or hollow. Without contents. Empty of ideas or intelligence. Devoid of significance. Devoid of substance or meaning. Empty-headed. Void of logic. Meaningless.

> • *Considering some of the* ***vacuous*** *comments made in the meeting, it is obvious they have no idea what should be done next.*

> • *A* ***vacuous*** *expression formed on her face.*

> • *He made a* ***vacuous*** *attempt at apologizing for his indifference.*

VAGARY
(va **gare** e)

> *Noun.* An erratic action. An unpredictable occurrence. An unforeseen change. An unexpected change in a situation or person's behavior. A whim. A capricious action. An impulsive action.

> • *Living in this part of the country, you quickly become accustomed to the* ***vagaries*** *of the weather.*

> • *It is our objective to return the company to profitability, notwithstanding the current* ***vagaries*** *of a shifting economic climate.*

VANDERBILT, CORNELIUS
United States financier (1794–1877). He began his business career at the age of sixteen when

he borrowed $100 to purchase a boat to start a transport and freight service between New York and Staten Island. He charged eighteen cents per trip. From that humble beginning, he went on to build one of the largest steamboat companies in the world. Later, he began acquiring railroads and in the process amassed great wealth. He was not well known for his philanthropic activities, but did provide a million dollars to help fund Vanderbilt University. He left the bulk of his estate to his son, William, the value of which was slightly over $100 million in 1877.

VANGUARD
(van gard)

Noun. The lead division or unit of an army. More commonly, it is used to describe the leading position in any field, movement or trend. The forefront. The leading or cutting edge. Anyone or any group occupying a foremost position. A group or an individual that brings new and innovative ideas to a given field.

• *Because of his mastery of both the tenor and soprano saxophones, his complex chord structures and the vibrant tones of his music, John Coltrane occupies a unique position in the* **vanguard** *of modern jazz.*

• *The Catcher in the Rye was written by J. D. Salinger and was first published in 1945. The unique writing style of the book was considered avant-garde by some and bizarre by others, but was widely read and widely acclaimed and thrust Salinger into the* **vanguard** *of American literary giants.*

VAPID
(**vap** id)

Adj. **Dull. Uninteresting. Flat. Lacking zest or flavor. Insipid. Colorless. Boring and lifeless. Without spirit or animation. Bland. Lacking significance or liveliness. Not stimulating. Not exciting.**

• *At the party, he became trapped in a conversation with a **vapid** woman who was more interested in how she looked than in what she said.*

• *The book began with a **vapid** account of his formative years. Eventually, it became so tedious that she refused to finish reading it.*

VEHEMENTLY
(**vay** uh ment lee)

Adv. **Fervently. Ardently. Passionately. Marked by forceful energy. Intensely. Furiously and emphatically. With strong convictions. Vigorously.**

• *The two board members **vehemently** despised each other, and as a result, they rarely agreed on many of the issues.*

• *The senator was visibly upset as he clenched the microphone to **vehemently** deny the accusations made against him.*

VENAL
(**vee** nul)

Adj. **Willing to sell one's services or influ-**

ence for money. Amenable to accepting a bribe. Corruptible. Purchasable. Open to persuasion for money or other valuable considerations. Able to be bought.

• *The political system in this small Middle Eastern country is so* **venal** *that influence peddling is widespread.*

Do not confuse venal with "venial" (vee nee al). "Venial" is an adjective that means minor or petty. That which is easily excused. Minor faults or transgressions. Catholicism holds that a venial sin does not deprive the soul of divine grace whereas a mortal sin does. Thus, "venial" is that which is "pardonable," or "condonable."

• *We knew he was inclined to be loud and somewhat obtrusive, but in light of his other qualities, we felt they were only* **venial** *shortcomings.*

VICARIOUS
(vi **care** e us)

Adj. The primary meaning is pertaining to a vicar, a substitute or deputy. Delegating to another as in "vicarious power." In the legal environment you have vicarious liability. This occurs when one person is liable for the negligent actions or activity of another. Much like an employer could be vicariously liable for the actions of its employees or a parent vicariously liable for the actions of a child. The more common usage is as a reference to receiving or experiencing something in place of another. Feeling or undergoing some experience as if you were taking part in the experience yourself. An imaginative participation in the experience of another.

• *Watching his sons play sports has always been a source of* **vicarious** *enjoyment for him.*

• *Because they went into such detail on the activities of each day, she was able to* **vicariously** (adverbial form) *experience their trip to Europe.*

VICISSITUDE
(vuh **sis** uh tude)

Noun. **A change. A variation. Evolved from one state to a variation of the original. A natural alteration in nature or human affairs. A mutation. A shift in what has been the case. Something different that occurs in due course or with time.**

• *Because a college career normally takes place over a four to five year period of time, it is very difficult to prepare a young person for the many* **vicissitudes** *of college life.*

• *It is astonishing to think they have remained so emotionally close through the* **vicissitudes** *of forty years of marriage.*

VILIFY
(**vill** uh fy)

Verb. **To slander. To malign. To speak evil of. To debase or degrade. To disparage or disgrace. To spread negative information. To defame. To cast aspersions (injurious statements).**

• *Many Americans **vilified** the French for the position they took on the United States' involvement in Iraq.*

• *Resist the temptation to **vilify** those you find offensive by remembering the advice of your parents: "If you can't say something good about someone—don't say anything."*

✪   The opposite of "vilify" is "praise," or "extol."

VINDICATE
(**vin** duh **kate**)

Verb. **To show to be blameless. To show to be correct. To prove to be valid. To exonerate. To be cleared of a charge. To provide justification. To confirm or substantiate with results or proof.**

• *Some evolutionists have claimed that the Human Genome Map proves man evolved from lower animals and thus **vindicates** Darwin's evolutionary theories.*

• *While many at the start doubted the efficacy of your sales strategy, its success was its real **vindication*** **(noun form).**

VIRULENT
(**veer** u lent)

Adj. **The primary meaning is actively poisonous. Deadly. Having the ability to cause a disease. Extremely toxic as a "virulent poison." Damaging. Deleterious. That which can overcome bodily defense mechanisms. Venomous.**

• *An incredibly **virulent** strain of flu has been isolated and blamed for a number of recent deaths in the Gulf Coast area.*

The secondary meaning of virulent is hostile. Intensely bitter. Spiteful. Extremely acrimonious. Full of malice. Antagonistic.

• *While she claims no political affiliation, she has for years been a **virulent** critic of the United States' foreign trade policy.*

VITIATE
(**vish** e ate)

Verb. **Primarily, it means to impair the quality of. To make faulty. To reduce the value of. To mar or contaminate. To blemish or tarnish. To weaken. To make defective.**

• *The CEO advised the middle management group to provide their direct reports with a free and unconstrained environment in which to work, one free of stringent guidelines and over-controlling rules that tend to **vitiate** young minds.*

Socially, the word means to corrupt morally. To spoil. To debase. To deflower. Legally, it is a term meaning to invalidate. To make void. To destroy the binding force of a legal instrument. To annul.

• *The new evidence presented in court **vitiated** her previous testimony.*

VIVACIOUS
(vi **vay** shus)

> *Adj.* **Lively. Spirited. Animated. Active and energetic. Sparkling. Idiomatically, "full of life." Expressive and enthusiastic.**

> • *She was tall and blonde and sported a pair of laughing, green eyes that did their part in making her one of the most* **vivacious** *young women on campus.*

> **The noun form of "vivacious" is "vivacity" (vi vass a tee), which is the state or quality of being "vivacious."**

> • *Her* **vivacity** *was her calling card.*

✪   The opposite of "vivacious" is "languid," or "torpid."

VIVIFY
(**viv** uh **fy**)

> *Verb.* **To give life to. To render lively. To give vitality or energy. To energize. To make more striking. To brighten. To quicken or to intensify. To stimulate or perk up. To enliven.**

> • *During a televised football game, the role of the color commentator is to* **vivify** *the broadcast with his knowledge and understanding of the game.*

> • *The spring rains* **vivified** *the grasslands at the base of the mountain range.*

VOCIFEROUS
(vo **sif** er us)

> *Adj.* **Vocal. Clamorous. So loudly it compels attention. Conspicuously loud. Offensively loud. Noisy. Strident. Boisterous. Shouting in a determined way.**

> • *The new legislation led to **vociferous**, but generally non-violent opposition.*

> • *He was an unpopular candidate, and the **vociferous** crowds that lined the streets made their feelings known as they continued to taunt him.*

✪   The opposite of "vociferous" is "quiet."

VOLUBLE
(**vol** u bul)

> *Adj.* **Talkative. Verbose. Long-winded. Characterized by a continual flow of words. Garrulous. Speaking incessantly. Loquacious. Chatty. Glib. Given to use many words.**

> • *His **voluble** style makes him a perfect candidate for the host of the late night talk show.*

> • *She was continually irritated by her **voluble** co-workers who frequently interrupted her productive time.*

> • *He quickly informed them that he would not listen to **voluble** excuses for poor performance.*

✪   The opposite of "voluble" is "taciturn," or "quiet."

WAIVE
(wave)

>*Verb.* To relinquish. To give up. To not claim. To give up a right or claim. To reject. To forfeit. It also means to not enforce something or to put restrictions aside. To cause a rule to not be put in effect.

>• *The charges were **waived**, since it was discovered that the bank made the accounting error.*

>• *His tuition costs were lowered once the university agreed to **waive** the non-resident charges.*

>• *She **waived** her right to remain silent.*

✪   The opposite of "waive" is "to put in force," or "implement."

WALKER CUP

>A golf tournament held every two years matching male amateurs from the United States against male amateurs from Great Britain and Ireland. The tournament was instituted in 1922 by George Herbert Walker, a former President of the United States Golf Association and maternal grandfather to George Herbert Walker Bush, who became the 41st President of the United States.

WANE
(wane)

>*Verb/Noun.* As a verb it means to diminish. To decrease or get smaller. To begin to disappear. To

fade. To dwindle. To decrease in intensity, power, importance, etc. To draw to a close.

• *As more and more scientific data was gathered and analyzed, the popularity and validity of his philosophical tenets began to* **wane**.

As a noun it means a gradual decrease in power, size, influence, etc.

• *With economic downturns appearing both domestically and abroad, his fortunes were on the* **wane**.

✪   The opposite of "wane" is "swell," or "get larger."

WANTON
(**won** ten)

Adj. Malicious. Reckless. Something done without reason or justification. Something done to cause harm. Inhumane. Something willful and unprovoked. Without motive. Uncalled-for.

• *The police investigators at the scene described it as a* **wanton** *destruction of human life.*

The word also means lacking in moral rectitude. Sexually unrestrained. Lewd. Lascivious. Lustful or sensual. Sexual behavior without inhibitions.

• *It broke his heart when he was told of the* **wanton**, *unbridled behavior of his only daughter.*

WARY
(**ware** e)

> *Adj.* Cautions. Vigilant. Circumspect. Openly distrustful. Suspicious. Attentive. Careful. Guarded against deception. Mindful. Prudently alert.

> • *As his father had told him many times—**be wary of the man who feels compelled to tell you how honest he is**.*

> • *There are those who believe that Microsoft is **wary** of Linux and the open-source philosophy since it could hinder Microsoft's ability to control the server market.*

✪   The opposite of "wary" is "careless."

WATERSHED
(**wau** ter **shed**)

> *Noun.* Topographically, it is a ridge of high land or a crest line that divides two rivers or lakes. A water parting. The Continental Divide is a watershed. It also refers to an area or basin that collects rain and snow that eventually drains into a river, stream or lake. Metaphorically, the word is widely used to indicate a critical point that affects future events. A turning point. An event or point in time that represents an historical change of course.

> • *The attack of 9/11 on the World Trade Center was an historic **watershed** in the United States' war on terrorism*

> • *The small Middle Eastern country's participation*

*with the United States–led coalition against Iraq was a dramatic **watershed** in its diplomatic relations with the West.*

WHIMSICAL
(**wim** zuh kul)

> *Adj.* **Fanciful. Unusual. Quaint. Determined by inclination rather than by reason. Imaginative. Quirky and impulsive. Capricious. Coming from a natural feeling or impulse.**

> • *Many times his decisions seem neither deliberate nor well thought out, but more **whimsical** in nature.*

> • *Her **whimsical** spending habits occasionally infuriated her husband.*

> ✪　The opposite of "whimsical" is "predictable."

WINSOME
(**win** sum)

> *Adj.* **Engaging. Pleasant. Endearing. Charming and attractive. Winning. Appealing, especially because of innocent or child-like qualities. Pleasing. Captivating.**

> • *She gained complete control of the review group by demonstrating the capabilities of the system in a witty and **winsome** manner.*

> ✪　The opposite of "winsome" is "repulsive," or "disgusting."

258

WOEFULLY
(**wo** ful lee)

Adv. **Involving woe or distress. Dolefully. Distressfully. Deplorably. Mournfully or lamentably. Sadly.**

• *After a review of all of the presentations, he quickly determined that the technical training they had received was **woefully** inadequate.*

• *There were many clamoring for an overhaul of the selection procedure by which American golfers are chosen to compete in the Ryder Cup matches after the Americans' **woefully** poor performance against the Europeans.*

WREST
(**rest**)

Verb. **To twist or turn. To move or force by a violent movement. To extract. To wring or squeeze. To pull out or take out. To take control. To obtain with effort or force. To remove.**

• *There is a movement underway to **wrest** control of the city government from corrupt and self-serving political machines.*

• *By committing so many blunders in the final minutes of the game, they literally **wrested** defeat from the jaws of victory!*

XENOPHOBIA
(**zen** uh **foe** be uh)
> *Noun.* A fear or deep dislike of foreigners.

YELLOW JOURNALISM
> This is a journalistic style that employs the use of scandalous, lurid or sensational stories to attract readership. It represents sensationalism over factual reporting. While it still exists today with tabloid journalism and some televised journalism, it reached staggering heights in the late 19th Century when stories were written with a careless disregard for the truth. The stories oftentimes exploited, distorted or exaggerated the news. At times, they were completely fabricated for the sake of attracting readership. The name is derived from cartoons called the Yellow Kid that appeared in the *New York World*, a newspaper noted for sensationalism. Ironically, the *New York World* during this time was owned by Joseph Pulitzer, whose legacy includes the endowment of a fund that awards Pulitzer Prizes annually to twenty-one fields of endeavor, some of which are in Journalism.

ZEALOUS
(**zel** us)
> *Adj.* Filled with zeal. Enthusiastic. Fervent. Passionate and spirited. Intense or unreserved enthusiasm toward a purpose or activity. Avid. Keenly interested. Ardent.

> • *He was a **zealous** advocate of decentralizing the*

*operations of the corporation by giving the field man-
agers more local control.*

• *She was a **zealous** art collector with many fine works
of art.*

ZENITH
(**zee** nith)

Noun. **In astronomy, it is a point in the celestial
hemisphere directly overhead of an observer and
diametrically opposite its lowest point (the nadir).
More commonly, the word is used to indicate the
highest point, summit or culmination point. The
highest level obtainable. The height of success or
prosperity. The apex or pinnacle.**

• *Once elected Chairman of the Board, he had reached
the **zenith** of his business career.*

• *To be awarded the Nobel Prize for medicine was the
zenith of her achievements.*

ZOÖPHOBIA
(**zoo** uh **foe** be uh)

Noun. **An intense fear of animals.**

A Few Guidelines On Writing

One of the more interesting aspects of the English language is its existence within a constant state of modification. New words are added every year, older words are deemed archaic, and words initially considered slang are accepted as proper form. It also includes the introduction of newly created words spawned by industry changes and inventions. Through this process, however, the language has suffered, and it is reflected in the quality of the non-fictional writing being produced today.

While there are a number of factors spurring this decline, one of the areas most culpable is the Internet. An in-depth discussion of this phenomenon is beyond the scope of this project, but a few observations relative to the Internet may shed some light. Without question, the Internet is one of the most significant developments of the Twentieth Century. The volume of information available is mind numbing, not to mention the speed at which it can be accessed. Information can be disseminated quickly to large numbers of people. Millions of emails are sent and received daily. The Internet gives users permission to write to each other as though it were a conversation between friends. Text messaging and instant messaging, ladened with initials and abbreviations, have added to the phenomena. The tone of these communications is loose and informal with little thought given to clarity or succinctness—all in the interest of speed.

No one can argue the benefits of such capability, but oftentimes these communications are loaded with clutter and ambiguity. Initials and industry jargon abound. Far too often they contain incomplete sentences and even omit the standard conventions of the English language such as syntax, spelling, punctuation, verb tense, and capitalization. The result of which is to render these messages confusing and sometimes unintelligible. There is the story of the president of a $10 billion corporation with over 70,000 employees worldwide who sent emails using the lower case "i" when referring to himself. It seemingly represented either a high order of carelessness or a massive ego defying tradition and convention. Regardless, it helped in giving the employees tacit permission to pay little heed to the quality of their communications. Unfortunately, this sort of carelessness becomes habitual and carries over to other areas besides email. It is one reason why it is found in virtually all forms of communications.

Sentences depend on clarity of construction to communicate effectively. Proper grammar and the use of words that accurately convey your thoughts are arrows in the quiver of a good communicator.

When creating non-fictional prose such as typing an email, preparing a report, writing an essay, composing a letter, or drafting a sales proposal, the following guidelines will greatly enhance the effectiveness of your material:

USE THE ACTIVE VOICE
The use of an active verb in a sentence means the subject of the sentence is acting upon someone

or something. The subject is doing something. A passive verb means the subject is being acted upon in the sentence. It is the recipient of the action. While the passive voice is certainly an acceptable form, typically the active voice creates better prose. Consider the following examples:

(Passive)
  • *The ball was hit by Leo.*

(Active)
  • *Leo hit the ball.*

The use of the active voice tightens up the sentence and makes it crisp and to the point.

AVOID COLLOQUIALISMS AND CLICHÉS
Colloquialisms are informal words or expressions used more in conversation than in formal speech or writing. They are not indicative of vulgar or incorrect usage. They are words or phrases used in everyday speech rather than in expository prose. Words like "drag" to indicate something that is boring or "no-brainer" as a reference to something that requires little thought should be avoided. In addition, contractions such as "isn't" and "don't" are colloquial and should not be included in more formal writing. You should take a similar stance on colloquial phrases such as, "Give it a hundred and ten percent," or "Our backs are against the wall."
Much the same could be said for the use of clichés in your writing. Clichés are phrases, ideas or expressions that have been so over used they have lost their original forcefulness. They are typically trite and

over-worn statements that show little originality or creativity. Avoid phrases such as, "to knuckle under," or "fall through the cracks," or "making money hand over fist." Even the phrase, "it was as bright as the sun," may not reside on Cliché Street, but it is certainly in the neighborhood. And, of course, avoid at all costs such clichéd similes as, "hungry as a bear," or "ran like a deer."

WHEN TO USE A SEMICOLON

A semicolon should join two closely related independent clauses that are not joined by a conjunction like "and" or "but." It indicates that both clauses are bound together more closely than if they were separated by a period. The first word following the semicolon is never capitalized unless it is a proper noun.

> • *I love to read his books; his stories are always so intricate and involved.*

Note that a conjunction could be used between the two clauses.
> • *I love to read his books, because his stories are always so intricate and involved.*

Note also that it is perfectly acceptable to construct two separate sentences.
> • *I love to read his books. His stories are always so intricate and involved.*

In this case, the first example is preferred since it shows a closer relationship between the two clauses. Additionally, the sentence is more tightly constructed and thus more forceful.

WHEN TO USE A COLON

Use a colon following an independent clause to introduce a list of items or for amplification. The use of a colon indicates to the reader that what follows is closely related to the first part of the sentence.

(For a list of items)
> • *His success was fashioned by three attributes: his desire to succeed, his insightfulness, and his ability to work with others.*

(For amplification)
> • *She suffered from strong feelings of resignation: there was little she could do to alleviate the burden of her situation.*

WHEN TO USE QUOTATION MARKS

Quotation marks are also called quotes and are used in modern English to show dialogue and quoted material. They are to be used in titles of shorter works like short fiction, poetry, films, and articles in magazines and journals.

When using a quotation in your text, a comma precedes the first quotation mark and the first letter of the quote is capitalized. The final quotation mark is placed outside the period.
> • *Will Rogers once said, "The income tax has made liars out of more Americans than golf."*

When something is quoted inside an existing quote, use single quotation marks.
> • *"The most famous movie quote of all time is from the movie classic, "Gone With The Wind", when Rhett*

Butler said, 'Frankly my dear, I don't give a damn,' and promptly walked out the door.'

Put titles of poems and titles of articles from magazines and journals in quotes.
• We had an opportunity to read several poems last night, one of which was Walt Whitman's, "O Captain! My Captain!"

Avoid Ending Sentences With A Preposition

A preposition is one of a set of function words used with nouns and pronouns (the objects of prepositions) to form a prepositional phrase that shows their relationship to another part of the sentence. Some of the more common prepositions are:

Across	Against	Among	Before
Below	Between	Except	For
From	In	Into	Inside
Of	On	Over	Since
To	Toward	Under	Upon
Until	With	Within	Without

Some grammarians will argue that since prepositions are meant to come before their objects, e.g., "He left *with* his sister," you should never end a sentence with a preposition. However, it is becoming more prevalent and acceptable for writers to end sentences with a preposition. For example, there may be no better way to write, "We have much to be thankful for." While this particular sentence is grammatically correct, there are still a number of readers who find it quite annoying to see a sentence ended with a preposition. As a writer, you need to keep the interests of your reader at heart. If you want to avoid the possibility of offending someone, usually all it takes is a little thoughtful editing.

Consider the following sentence:
- *"This is the table I would like to sit at."*

This could be changed to:
- *"This is the table at which I would like to sit."*

While the second version does not end in a preposition, it is awkward and stilted and takes more words to get the same point across. As stated above, a simple rewrite may be the answer.
- *"This is the table where I would like to sit."*

Or better yet, you could use a simple declarative sentence that expresses the thought clearly and succinctly.
- *"I would like to sit at this table."*

Winston Churchill may have been one of those individuals who did not object to ending a sentence with a preposition. A civil servant once wrote an awkwardly constructed sentence just to avoid ending the sentence with a preposition. This prompted Mr. Churchill to pen a humorous note in the margin: "This is the sort of English up with which I will not put."

Do Not Hesitate
To Rewrite A Sentence

When beginning a composition of any length, one of the biggest mistakes you can make is to try to create a worthwhile final product on the first attempt.

This rarely happens. A proven approach is to simply begin writing either from an outline or from notes you have created. Get your thoughts and ideas on paper. In this manner, you are focused more on what you want to express rather than how to express it. Sentences can then be changed and paragraphs can be moved upon rewrite. You will find that this approach not only improves the quality of what you have written, but will significantly enhance the cadence and flow of your composition.

There are times when you can become hopelessly perplexed in attempting to make a sentence convey your exact thoughts or ideas. Sometimes what you have written just doesn't sound good to the ear. It probably means you are trying to make the sentence carry a greater load than it can bear. You have put too many thoughts or ideas into what you have written and in the process have flawed the syntax of the sentence. Rather than labor endlessly over its construction, a simple rewrite that breaks it into two or more sentences is usually the answer.

There are also occasions when a sentence you have written is so weak it is better to discard it completely. You will find that you can save a great deal of time simply by starting over rather than continuing to polish a stone that is never going to shine.

Using Abbreviations

Acronyms and initialisms have entered the English language as a means of saving time and effort when referring to various organizations or technical terms. They are less cumbersome for the reader and are often used in any form of communication where it is necessary to continually refer to the organization or term. In modern English there are several conventions that have been generally accepted. When the name first appears, spell it out in its entirety with the abbreviation in parenthesis or brackets: for example, The American Civil Liberties Union [ACLU]. Thereafter, use just the abbreviation. In the past it was commonplace to use periods (full stops) following each letter, but that is beginning to change depending on which published style guide you choose to follow. Certain words, however, require full stops. The United States should be abbreviated to U.S. and not US because the second form spells another word.

The difference between an acronym and an initialism is one of pronunciation. For example, NATO (North Atlantic Treaty Organization) is pronounced, "nay toe" as SARS (Severe Acute Respiratory Syndrome) is pronounced, "sarz." The individual letters are not pronounced. With intialisms, the individual letters are pronounced as in "CD" (compact disk) or PC (personal computer). There are many acronyms and initialisms in use today. A few of the more common are:

Acronyms
Radar - Radio Detection And Ranging
Sonar - Sound Navigation Ranging
Laser - Light Amplification by Simulated Emission of Radiation
Scuba - Self-Contained Underwater Breathing Apparatus
Wasp - White Anglo-Saxon Protestant
Aids - Acquired Immune Deficiency Syndrome

Initialisms

e.g. **(Latin)** *exempli gratia* **(for example)**
• Nutritional studies have shown that foods that are good for you contain high amounts of fiber, **e.g.**, fruits, vegetables and whole grains.
Note: Always place a comma before and after e.g.

i.e. **(Latin)** *id est* **(that is)**
• Attendance is discretionary, **i.e.**, it is up to you if you want to attend.
Note: Always place a comma before and after i.e.

etc. **(Latin)** *et cetera* **(and so on) also (and other unspecified things)**
• Before we leave for the campsite, we should pack clothes, food, flashlights, eating utensils, **etc.**

et al. **(Latin)** *et alii* **(and others)**
• We need to invite each member of the team including the coaches, the trainers, the staff, **et al**.

et seq. **(Latin)** *et sequens* **(and those that follow)**
• A comprehensive description of the events that occurred can be found on page 20, **et seq**.

ibid. **(Latin)** *ibidem* **(in the same place)**–typically used in footnotes.

Common Latin Phrases
Ad infinitum–(to infinity) or (going on forever)
Ad nauseam–(to the point of nausea)
Ad valorem–(according to the value) or (in proportion to the value)

De facto–(in fact) or (as things really are)
Ex libris–(from the books or library)
Ex post facto–(after the fact) or (that which is done afterward)
Habeas corpus–(you must have the body)
In vitro–(in glass)
Ipso facto–(by the fact itself)
Magnum opus–(a great work)
Non sequitur–(it does not follow)
Per diem–(per day)
Per se–(by itself) or (in itself)
Quid pro quo–(this for that) or (an exchange of one thing for another)
Terra firma–(solid ground)

Care should be exercised when using acronyms, initialisms, or various Latin phrases. While they are useful tools in the hands of a writer, you want to avoid irritating the reader. Excessive use of *et cetera*, for example, could convey one of two things—you are either too lazy to complete the details or you really don't have anything more to add, but you want the reader to think you do. These impressions you want to avoid.

Additionally, excessive use of Latin phrases or foreign language phrases can not only be sometimes difficult for the reader, it can give the appearance that you are either just showing off or trying to make the material appear more scholarly than it really is. Again, these are impressions you want to avoid.

BITS AND PIECES...

[Farther vs. Further]–the easiest way to use the correct word is to remember that there is a "far" in the word "farther," indicating distance. *"It is farther to New York than it is to Miami."*

Use "further" to show "more" or "to a greater extent." *"Her statements provided further evidence of his innocence."*

[Advisor vs. Adviser]–can be spelled either way and have identical meanings.

[Fewer vs. Less]–use "fewer" with things you can count like *"fewer lights"* or *"fewer books."* Use "less" for things you cannot count like *"less physical"* or *"less motivated."*

[Between vs. Among]–use "between" when writing about two people or two things. Use "among" when considering three or more people or things.

[All Right vs. Alright]–use "all right" to indicate everything is satisfactory. "Alright" is non-standard usage.

[Its vs. It's]–"its" is a possessive pronoun that shows ownership (possession), as do other possessive pronouns like "his," "hers," "mine," "yours," "theirs," and "ours." For example, *"The committee was asked to reconsider its decision."*

On the other hand, "it's" is a contraction of either "it is," or "it has" as in, *"It's a beautiful day,"* or *"It's been nice talking with you."*

[Once And A While]–the correct expression is, *"Once In A While."*

[Theirs vs. There's vs. They're]–as indicated above, "theirs" is a possessive pronoun.

However, "there's" is a contraction meaning "there is" as in, *"There's more to this story than meets the eye."*

"They're" is also a contraction meaning "they are" as in *"They're ready to go."*

It should be noted that "their's" is non-existent.

[Which vs. Who vs. That]—when using any of these words, follow these basic guidelines:

Only use "which" when referring to things as in, *"These are candles which I will place on the mantel."*

Only use "who" when referring to people as in, *"This is the man who will be our guide."*

The word "that" is a little more versatile. It normally refers to things as in, *"Here is the car that I will drive."* But, it can also be used to refer to a class of people as in, *"I think this is the team that will win the championship."*

FINAL THOUGHTS

It has been said that within each of us is an inner voice that has been shaped and molded by our environment, by those around us, and by what we have learned in the course of our lives. It is this inner voice that we call upon to express our thoughts and ideas. Learning the information contained herein will enhance the breadth and quality of your inner voice and ultimately make your written material more forceful and effective. As part of the learning process, you should also equip your personal library with an unabridged dictionary and a guidebook on the rules of grammar—both invaluable tools for the writer.

Finally, you will write more clearly and concisely by being attentive to just a few grammatical rules, by removing all superfluous words, and by using only those words that correctly express the thoughts you are attempting to convey. Before you begin any composition, organize your thoughts with either an outline, or simply jot down a few notes on the major points you want to make. Avoid ambiguity. Be direct and succinct. Remember, you are conveying your thoughts to the mind of the reader—don't let the words get in the way.

Contributors

A significant feature of *The American Fact•ionary* is its "openness." If you know of obscure yet interesting facts, compatible words, or ones with curious etymologies that you feel should be included, you are encouraged to submit them to the author at www.theamericanfactionary.com. All submissions will be thoroughly evaluated. If your submission is accepted, you will be notified immediately, and the entry together with the proper credits will be included in subsequent editions of *The American Fact•ionary*.

The following is a list of those individuals who have contributed to this publication.

Aphorism	*Douglas McKnight, La Jolla, California*
Bellwether	*Phyllis Lambert, Stillwater, Oklahoma*
Complement	*Dave Erdman, Dallas, Texas*
Crocodile Tears	*Mike McCourt, Galveston, Texas*
Duplicity	*Lawrence Testa, Hugo, Oklahoma*
Epithet	*Allison Kramer, Atlanta, Georgia*
Fortnight	*Kristy Lambert, Kansas City, Kansas*
Golf Links	*Tom Melby, Broadway, Virginia*
Jet Stream	*Dick Weir, Lafayette, California*
Mach Number	*Tim Lowery, San Diego, California*
P's & Q's	*Joe Gaukler, Dallas, Texas*
Power of Attorney	*Jim Love, Tulsa, Oklahoma*
Quixotic	*Dr. Robert D. Culp, Northglenn, Colorado*

Spoonerism	*Vicki Edge, Dallas, Texas*
Ubiquitous	*William Testa, Montgomery, Alabama*
Yellow Journalism	*Cindy Hultgren, New Albany, Ohio*

Index

The Index has been categorically divided to assist you in the composition of any form of written communication. If you have a writing assignment (writing a report, drafting a proposal or preparing an essay), simply find the broad category under which your topic or any portion of your topic falls and review the words listed.

The words will not only allow you to think conceptually, they will actively stimulate the mind. Once stimulated, the human mind acts as a creative juggernaut capable of broadening areas of consideration and opening new vistas of thought not initially contemplated. The result is a more expansive and more enriched composition.

Location

Interesting Facts

A Few Guidelines On Writing

ABOUT THE AUTHOR

Upon graduation from college, Mr. Testa served as a Lieutenant (jg) aboard the aircraft carrier, USS Bon Homme Richard (CVA-31), where he was assigned the position of Public Information Officer. He later served as the speechwriter and press officer for the Commandant of the 13th Naval District in Seattle, Washington.

In the private sector, he began his business career in Dallas, Texas with IBM Corporation that eventually led to his appointment as Branch Manager of IBM in Huntsville, Alabama. He returned to Dallas and joined the commercial real estate firm of Cushman & Wakefield of Texas, Inc. as Director of Branch Operations and was later promoted to Vice President & Branch Manager. The last five years of his business career he served as the Strategic Alliances Manager for the Informix Corporation.

Mr. Testa is retired and currently resides in Dallas where he has already begun work on subsequent editions of *The American Fact•ionary*.

TATE PUBLISHING & *Enterprises*

Tate Publishing is committed to excellence in the publishing industry. Our staff of highly trained professionals, including editors, graphic designers, and marketing personnel, work together to produce the very finest books available. The company reflects the philosophy established by the founders, based on Psalms 68:11,

"THE LORD GAVE THE WORD AND GREAT WAS THE COMPANY OF THOSE WHO PUBLISHED IT."

If you would like further information, please call
1.888.361.9473
or visit our website
www.tatepublishing.com

TATE PUBLISHING & *Enterprises*, LLC
127 E. Trade Center Terrace
Mustang, Oklahoma 73064 USA